ECONOMICS OF FUELWOOD PRODUCTION IN WASTELANDS

ABOUT THE AUTHOR

DR. R.D. SHARMA holds M.Sc. (Ag.), Ph.D. degree in Agricultural Economics and specializes in farm economy research, rural development and project evaluation. He has long working experience under different capacities in India, Tanzania and Iraq. He is consultant to various organisations in Government of India and on the panel of experts in different U.N. bodies. He has travelled widely in Africa, Middle East, South and East Asia under various assignments.

Dr. Sharma is the Founder-Director, Centre for Economic and Development Research, Ghaziabad and is associated with a number of academic institutions. He has to his credit over fifty publications.

ECONOMICS
OF
FUELWOOD PRODUCTION
IN
WASTELANDS

R.D. SHARMA
Director, Centre for Economic and
Development Research
Ghaziabad

CONCEPT PUBLISHING COMPANY, NEW DELHI 110059

ISBN 81-7022-436-5

First Published 1992

Published and Printed by
Ashok Kumar Mittal
Concept Publishing Company
A/15-16, Commercial Block, Mohan Garden
NEW DELHI-110059

Lasertypeset by
Microtech Advance Printing Systems (Pvt.) Ltd.
H-13, Bali Nagar
NEW DELHI 110015

PREFACE

The Indian wastelands, forming a large part of the total geographical area, can gradually be brought under productive use. The country has acquired the suitable techniques and skills for restoration the productivity of these lands through afforestation and especially the fuelwood plantations. Thus the increasing demand of fuelwood and constraints of its supply could be meet out if most promising species are grown on these rehabilitated wastelands. The rehabilitation and cultivation of plantations on these lands for fuelwood production require large sums of financial resources. Unless specific amount on the cost of production of the needed species are not known it would be a crude exercise to estimate the total expenditure and measurable benefits expected from the programme.

This study is an attempt to compile the various data on cost structure for the development of man-made forestry/fuelwood plantations. An exercise has been made to calculate the cost of per sapling raised at the nurseries. Fourteen most promising species suitable to be included in the fuelwood plantations programme have been identified for detailed calculations. The per hectare cost of plantations and benefit-cost ratios for various species under different climatic regions of the country have been dealt in detail.

The concept of energy cultivation has recently been taken up and Department of Non-Conventional Energy Sources, Ministry of Energy, Government of India, played a pioneer role for providing funds on the plantation projects (both under R & D and energy plantations) in different parts of the country. It was expected to get the major part of primary data from these projects on a set of tested schedules. Unfortunately this could not be possible. There had been many explanations and problems but the severe drought conditions prevailed during the years with high mortality rate of plants have been the prime. Almost in all the areas the poor performance on plantations was noticed and primary data could not be collected on the lines as was desired. Thus the main source of information for raising the plantations has been the secondary data.

The report has been divided into seven chapters. Chapter 1 deals the overall energy situation in India, place of fuelwood in total energy and needs for salvation from the scarcity of rural energy supply. Chapter 2 gives an idea of the concept of energy forestry and steps taken in to improve the availability of fuelwood through afforestation programme. Chapter 3 describes the wasteland areas in the country. Cost of producing the saplings at nurseries, marketing of fuelwood and fuelwood prices have been included in Chapter 4. The case studies on the cost of fuelwood plantations for number of species have been dealt in Chapter 5. In Chapter 6, the unit cost (per hectare) of plantation raised as described in the Chapter 5 and also from other resources have been dealt. Based on this information, the benefit-cost ratios also have been calculated in this chapter. The last chapter deals with the summary aspects besides emphasis has been given on some of the suggestions as for the salvation of the problem.

I owe special gratitude to many researchers and persons in the field from whose research papers, reports or discussion with whom have helped in completing this work. The discussions held with late Dr. O.P. Vimal at various times and his friendly attitude encouraged me a lot. I am thankful to Dr. P.H.V. Vasudeva Rao, Head, Centre for Bio-Resources, Institute for Coastal and Offshore Research, Visakhapatnam, Dr. V.J. Patel, Director, Jivajibhai Patel Agro-Forestry Centre, Kardej, Gujarat and Shri Mahendra Singh, Farm Manager, Central Dairy Farm, Aligarh. I am also thankful to Dr. H.L. Sharma, Dr. D.K. Khare, DNES for their co-operation and helping attitude throughout the period of the study and finally to all my colleagues at CEDR for their efforts in the compilation of the work.

R.D. SHARMA

CONTENTS

LIST OF TABLES

ANNEXURES

ABBREVIATIONS

Cal Val	:	Calorific Value; Stands for amount of energy being released by burning of the wood.
DNES	:	Department of Non-Conventional Energy Sources.
G.O.I.	:	Government of India
ha	:	Hectare
HDAF	:	High Density Agro Forestry
ICAR	:	Indian Council of Agriculture Research
kg	:	Kilogram
kWh	:	Kilowatt Hour
mt	:	metric tonne
MTCR	:	Million Tonnes of Coal Replacement
NCA	:	National Commission on Agriculture
NREP	:	National Rural Employment Programme
NRSA	:	National Remote Sensing Agency
NWDB	:	National Wasteland Development Board
pH	:	Degree of acidity and alkalinity. pH7 stands for neutral substance, pH7 to 14 stands for alkaline substance and pH1 to 7 for acidic substance
RLEGP	:	Rural Labour Employment Guarantee Programme

1

ENERGY SCENARIO AND THE FUELWOOD

The widespread scarcity of fossile fuel, coal and electricity has affected on the over all economic development of the developing countries. The increase in prices of imported petroleum products has put great strains on the balance of payments of these countries where economy cuts in the other programmes have widely been observed. Thus energy, the backbone of development, has become a critical input during the recent past. Energy, when it is attempted to study for its application for the formal economic method of analysis to what determines the choice of fuels is grouped as commercial and non-commercial. Coal, petroleum products, electricity, nuclear power etc. come under the commercial group and firewood, cow-dung, agricultural wastes etc. as non-commercial. Consumers of these energy also differ. Non-commercial consumers of energy are those who obtain their supply without paying cash for it, they simply gather it from their surroundings. Commercial consumers, on the other hand, pay for the requirements they use.

The rural areas are the worst affected of the shortages of energy and the rural population continues to depend on the inefficient non-commercial energy for meeting their energy requirements for subsistence and productive needs. This non-commercial energy consumption accounts up to 90 per cent of the energy used in the developing countries (F.A.O., 1983). The vast majority of this energy is collected by families for their own use partly because major proportion of the rural population is too poor to buy commercial energy. The production of this energy does not pass through any market channel. Since a major portion of the energy supply is secured by private efforts at a very low cost, the fiscal and administrative control on distribution make little impact in the rural areas. This unrestrained growth in the use of non-commercial energy resources has resulted in serious environmental problems including deforestation, soil erosion and loss of soil fertility.

The energy crisis in rural areas has been getting increasing attention from the policy-makers and the Seventh Five Year Plan (1985-1990) an attempt is being made to tackle this problem in a planned and integrated manner.

The distinctive features of energy situation in the country have been dealt in the present chapter.

The total and per capita production of the total energy in the country through different means of production is given in Table 1.1.

TABLE 1.1: Population and energy production in India

Year	Population million	Coal 1000 mt (kg)	Petroleum 1000 mt (kg)	Electricity million kWh (kWh)	Natural gas tetru-joule (megajoule)	Fuel wood 1000 cm (cm)
1962	449.64	5114	90	1789	—	85210
	per capita	11.37	0.20	3.98	—	.189
1967	505.08	5685	472	3159	21.2	93210
	per capita	11.26	0.93	6.25	0.042	.184
1972	563.49	6231	624	5350	57.7	103720
	per capita	11.06	1.11	9.49	0.102	.184
1977	625.82	8358	849	7614	4199	175303
	per capita	13.36	1.36	12.17	6.71	.280
1982	705.00	10693	1645	10832	7386	193984
	per capita	15.17	2.33	15.36	10.48	.275
1987	781.37	13839	2512	16508	22142	209163 (1986)
	per capita	17.71	3.21	21.13	28.34	.267

Source: U.N. Monthly Bulletin of Statistics, F.A.O. Year Book of Forest Products and self calculations.

Accordingly, except, fuelwood, there has been tremendous increase during the past 25 years in all the sources of energy production in India. In 1987 (1962) per capita energy production was as follows: Coal 17.71 (11.37) kg, petroleum 3.21 (0.20) kg, electricity 21.13 (3.98) kWh, natural gas 28.34 (nil) megajoule and fuelwood 0.267 (.189) cm.

The per capita consumption of commercial energy in India is only about one-eighth of the world average and this source of energy accounts for only a little over a half of total energy used. The rest of the requirements come from non-commercial resources. These non-commercial resources constitute over 90 per cent of the energy consumed in the rural areas where more than 75 per cent of the population lives. The rural sector contributes significantly to the low per capita consumption in India eventhough non-commercial energy consumption in absolute terms has been rising. Table 1.2 shows the sectorwise proportion and total units under each category of energy consumed.

TABLE 1.2: Totals and percentage in each form of energy

Energy/Sector	Total units	Percentage share				
		House-hold	Industry	Transport	Agricul-ture	Others
I *Commercial*						
Electricity (bkWh)	424.0	19.20	58.7	2.9	9.65	10.5
Coal (m. tonne)	188.0	7.45	85.6	2.7	—	2.8
Oil (m. tonne)	727.0	24.40	16.5	41.0	11.40	6.9
II *Non-Commercial (household & agriculture)*						
Fuelwood (m. tonne)	191.6	—	—	—	—	—
Dung cake (m. tonne)	105.0	—	—	—	—	—
Vegetable waste (mt)	59.0	—	—	—	—	—

Source: S.K. Chopra (1988).

Table 1.3 shows the percentage share of energy consumed within the each sector of energy.

The pattern indicates a rapid rise in the share of commercial energy in the agricultural sector, a dominance of electricity and coal in industry sector, and dominance of oil in transport sector. The household has increased its use of oil and electricity but still has fuelwood as the major source of energy in the rural areas. Several studies conducted in this regard confirm the trend. An earlier study conducted by NCAER in the late seventies for the pattern of household energy consumption in North India shows a following change over for a period of four years duration (Table 1.4).

TABLE 1.3: Percentage share within the sector in terms of energy

Energy	Household	Industry	Transport	Agriculture
Electricity	15.60	57.40	2.00	62.70
Coal	2.70	37.10	4.00	—
Oil	28.20	5.50	94.00	37.30
Fuelwood	34.80	—	—	—
Dungcake	8.00	—	—	—
Vegetable waste	10.70	—	—	—
Total	100.00	100.00	100.00	100.00

Source: S.K. Chopra (1988).

TABLE 1.4: Pattern of fuel consumption in rural areas of the northern region in 1975-76 and 1978-79

	1975-76	1978-79
Per capita consumption (kg)	199	204
Share of commercial fuel (%)	4.5	6.1
Per capita consumption of :		
Soft coke (kg)	0.5	0.4
Kerosene (l)	2.7	3.4
Electricity (kWh)	2.4	5.1
Firewood (kg)	119.6	153.1
Crop wastes (kg)	94.9	56.1
Charcoal (kg)	0.7	0.1
Dung cake (kg)	158.1	194.4
Per cent of fuel collected	80	89

Source: I. Natarajan (1980).

The above energy consumption pattern for households shows that dungcake, firewood and crop wastes form the major part in the northern parts of India. The per capita energy consumption in the households have increased by 2.5 per cent during the four years period. This pattern of energy consumption as can be assumed has more or less been at the same level in other parts of the country. The projected consumption of energy leads to calculate the requirement by 2000.

The calculated and projected share of energy consumption for the end of the century under major sectors is given in Table 1.5.

TABLE 1.5: Sectorwise share of energy consumption

Sectors	1979-80	1984-85	1989-90	2000	2000 (all sources percentage)
Household	15.7	18.2	14.23	21.78	37.50
Agriculture	9.4	9.8	10.36	5.60	4.70
Industry	38.2	36.4	55.00	39.00	32.10
Transport	32.8	31.4	16.80	25.60	20.40
Others	3.9	4.2	3.60	7.80	6.25

Source: S.K. Chopra (1988).

The consumption trend of energy under different sectors shows a vide range. Proportionately agriculture and transport have shown the down trend while industry at a static stage and others besides household upward trend. The household sector is seen to emerge as having an increasing share in energy use, both as a result of population increase and increase in the standard of living.

The Advisory Board on Energy (1985) has estimated the energy requirements by 2000 A.D. Table 1.6 gives the sectorwise breakup.

TABLE 1.6: Sectoral breakup of energy requirement by 2000 A.D.

Energy/Sector	Household	Industry	Transport	Agriculture
I. *Commercial*				
Electricity (billion kWh)	81.40	249.00	8.20	40.50
Coal (m. tonnes)	14.00	261.00	7.81	—
Oil (m. tonnes)	17.70	12.00	29.90	8.1
II. *Non-commercial*				
Fuelwood (m. tonnes)	191.60	—	—	—
Dungcake (m. tonnes)	105.00	—	—	—
Vegetable waste (m. tonnes)	59.00	—	—	—

Source: Report of the Advisory Board on Energy (1985).

The Advisory Board also have figured the 1984 and projected for 2000 the non-commercial energy consumption in rural India. Table 1.7 shows the projected non-commercial energy consumption in rural India.

The calculations of Table 1.7 show that though the share of non-commercial energy sources in the total has been coming down in percentage terms, their consumption has increased in absolute terms. In

1984 they account for 229 million tonnes of coal replacement (MTCR) and projected to be 280 MTCR in the year 2000 AD.

TABLE 1.7: Projected non-commercial energy consumption in rural India (MTCR Units)

Source	1984	Projected for 2000 AD
Fuelwood	95	182
Dungcake	96	42
Agricultural waste	38	56
Total	229	280

Source: Report of the Advisory Board on Energy (1985).

The calculations of Tables 1.7 show that though the share of non-commercial energy sources in the total has been coming down in percentage terms, their consumption has increased in absolute terms. In 1984 they account for 229 million tonnes of coal replacement (MTCR) and projected to be 280 MTCR in the year 2000 AD.

Fuelwood, among the non-commercial sources, is the main contributor of rural energy supply. It has remained the most important in non-commercial energy in the household sector, for cooking and heating, accounting for 68.5 per cent and 45.5 per cent of the total energy consumption in rural and urban areas respectively. Expectedly, therefore, there has been progressive rise in consumption of non-commercial energy, as a whole, and fuelwood, in particular. The Working Group on Energy Report (1979) has expressed that inspite of a slight decline of 4.8 per cent in the over-all use of non-commercial energy, in the decade 1965-75, the relative position of fuelwood (65 per cent of the total) has remained unchanged. Those people who think that wood is a fuel of the past; it has been gaining in importance steadily as a source of energy in developed countries particularly, importance as it is for the developing ones. Since there are several economic, social and environmental advantages occurring from non-commercial energy, it is receiving greater attention of policy makers, planners and funding agencies. India is not leg behind in the policy decisions. The projected figures for 2000 as are presented by the Advisory Board on Energy, fuelwood will remain unchanged in the ratio of 65: 35 among the total non-commercial energy.

Population growth and the continuing dependence on fuelwood in rural areas has led supply to fall too far behind demand. The decreasing forests, increased intensity of floods and droughts have added to the shortages. According to the Planning Commission estimates by the turn of century the demand of fuelwood would be about three times of the expected supply. Since the production of fuelwood has not been able to keep pace with the requirement, the prices of fuelwood during the past two decades in India have shown an abnormally high increase (also see Chapter 4). The fuelwood prices increased more steeply than the consumer price index. In many cases prices have doubled. Because of the increasing costs of petroleum products and other sources of commercial energy besides the supply constraints, the fuelwood prices can be expected to increase in real terms faster in the coming years.

The use of non-commercial fuels in the household sector is not simply a rural phenomenon, urban households also rely on these fuels and especially on wood and charcoal. While the use of commercial fuels are more common in the urban areas where incomes are higher and these fuels are more readily and cheaply available, non-commercial fuel use is extensive. Foley (1986) gives a comparative study at different locations in the less developed countries. Table 1.8 shows the relative prices of different fuels in the urban centres.

TABLE 1.8: Relative prices of different fuels in settled areas

Locations	Relative prices by weight			
	Wood	Charcoal	Kerosene	LPG
Bamako, Mali (1979)	1-1.7	5.3-6.0	—	—
Bangalore, India (1979-80)	1	2.2	5.5	7.8
New Delhi, India (1982)	1	—	3.6 (subsidized) 7.6 (unsubsidized)	—
Indonesia (1981)	1	18.4	5.2	21.9
Niamey, Niger (1983)	1	2.5	8.7	—
Nigeria (1983)	1-3.8	4.9	2.7-5.0	7.8
Senegal (1982)	1	2.5	8.7	1.5-3.1
Uganda (1982)	1	3.2	14.7	20.6
Yeman Arab Republic (1983)	1-2	1.6	1.0	1.0

Source: Gerald Foley (1986).

Table 1.8 provides a compilation of comparative price data for wood and conventional fuels expressed on an index basis for a number of countries. The price of wood is taken as base line in each case. The energy sources are shown as compared to fuelwood. Comparing the figures, the fuelwood is still a cheap source of energy in all parts of the world. These competitive lower prices of fuelwood have further shown the intensive use of fuelwoods as a main source of energy in the major consuming areas.

India leads the list of the fuelwood producing countries in the world but its per capita production is far behind many countries. The 1986 data have been analysed in Table 1.9.

TABLE 1.9: High fuelwood producing countries (1986)

Country	Fuelwood production (1000 cum)	World rank	Per capita production (cm/head)
India	209163	1	0.27
Indonesia	128879	2	0.77
Brazil	125033	3	0.90
China	103634	4	0.10
Nigeria	82539	5	0.84
U S A	78687	6	0.32
Ethiopia	33288	7	0.74
USSR	30400	8	0.11
Philippines	29835	9	0.53
Zaire	28834	10	0.91

Source: FAO: Year Book of Forest Products and self calculations.

Besides the production of fuelwood, India's total consumption is the highest among all the nations. El-Hinnawi (1983) has estimated India's consumption of fuelwood at 133 million tonnes per annum followed by Nigeria 49 m tonnes, Thailand 24.5 m tonnes, Kenya 22 m tonnes etc.

In urban areas the consumption of fuelwood is mainly for the domestic uses of cooking and water heating purposes. Other purposes although less important and varied in nature but consume a lot of fuelwood and that accounts to about 23 per cent of the total utilisation. Table 1.10 shows the results of the studies for fuelwood consumption carried out at Bangalore City.

The sourcewise consumption of fuelwood as indicated by the study shows that 77.5 per cent of the total goes for household purposes. The other main uses are in dye factories, backeries, hotels, industries and so on.

TABLE 1.10: Fuelwood consumption in Bangalore (tonnes)

Sl. No.	Consumer	Firewood		% of total consumption	End uses		
		Day	Year		Cooking	Water	Process
1.	Households	970.0	334,050	77.5	375	559	—
2.	Dye Factories	62.0	22,530	5.0	—	62	—
3.	Bakeries	55.0	20,075	4.4	55	—	—
4.	Hotels	48.0	17,520	3.8	48	—	—
5.	Industries	47.5	17,337	3.8	—	—	17.5
6.	Choultries	24..2	8,760	1.9	24	—	—
7.	Hostels	24.0	8,760	1.9	24	—	—
8.	Cremation Ground	10.0	3,650	0.8	—	—	—
9.	Canteens	4.5	1,642	0.4	4.5	—	—
10.	Road building	4.0	1,460	0.3	—	—	4
11.	Soap Factories	3.0	1,095	0.2	—	—	3
	Total	1,250.0	469,979	100%	530	657	64.5
				%	42	53	5

Source: A.D.N. Reddy and B.S. Reddy (1983).

ASTRA (1981) has conducted surveys in a group of villages in Karnataka. Results of these surveys reveal that energy consumed for cooking in these villages amounts to 8.0 GJ per capita per annum. This consumption of energy is comparable to the fuelwood demand for household cooking in other states too. The Report of the Working Group on Energy Policy, Planning Commission (1979) estimates that about 20 per cent of the total population lives in towns and cities and approximately 65 per cent of the urban households use fuelwood as a cooking fuel — this corresponds to about 30 million tonnes a year.

The latest report of the Advisory Board for Energy (1985) concludes that the fuelwood demand is going to be of the order of 300-330 million tonnes against the present level of 120-150 million tonnes. Nearly 70 per cent fuel wood demand pertains to rural sector. According to the Board, the fuelwood scenario in 2004 05 is likely to be as follows:

– Like to meet the fuelwood demand	:	Gujarat, Rajasthan, Madhya Pradesh, Himachal Pradesh, Kashmir and Maharashtra

– Likely to meet after

(i) All available land is planted	:	West Bengal, Bihar, Assam and Andhra Pradesh
(ii) Increasing forest cover and productivity of existing forests	:	Karnataka

– Not likely to meet : Uttar Pradesh & Tamil Nadu

– Acute shortages : Punjab, Haryana & Kerala

The fact of the chronic shortages of fuelwood for energy purposes in most parts of India is not doubted and rural people have often to travel greater and greater distances to collect fuelwood for their essential daily needs. Thus the growing shortages of wood fuels and also the supplies of other non-commercial fuels are the main factors that brings about change in needs. Therefore, a major policy goal in the national planning is to contain unrestrained use of fuelwood.

M.S. Swaminathan in the introduction to the Report of the Fuelwood Study Committee (1982) of the Planning Commission has pointed out, India is bestowed with abundant sunlight which provides enormous opportunities for harnessing this energy through the photosynthetic path way of bio-mass production. The Sixth Five Year Plan outlined a detailed strategy for self-reliance in the energy sector. The Plan had made a special provision for the establishment of energy plantation and emphasis has been given to harnessing the sources of energy to meet the energy requirements of rural communities. This can be done through a combination of programmes, involving :

(i) augmentation of supply;
(ii) conservation through efficient use, and;
(iii) provision of alternatives.

To sum up with the suggestions for the above programmes, followings are considered:

The demand and supply position has shown that the gap is ever widening and productivity per unit area/time is very low. Thus to circumvent the situation and the satisfy rural energy needs is to go in for a massive afforestation programme. The objective has to be that every village is able to meet its fuelwood, fodder and timber requirements by growing trees and shurbs on available land. For buffer stock all the degraded government lands/forests be planted for the fast growing species of fuelwood. Realising the importance, the Prime Minister in his broadcast to the nation on 5th January, 1985, emphasised to deforestation and suggested to bring five million hectares of land every year under fuelwood and fodder plantations. The key factors for this success will be the correct planting techniques and proper high yielding genotypes of the species that are adaptable on these degraded lands.

Many energy conservation technologies are currently in use or under development. Examples, range from biogas converters to high technology options such as photovoltaics where energy can be generated from sun light, but the high cost of that energy means that end use devices such as pumps must be designed for high efficiency. The devices like gasifier, wind mills, solar cookers etc. are already under use and experimental stage, requires further adaptability and resource adjustments. Smoke less chulhas have already been promoted in a number of clusters in the country.

With the context of the objectives of the present study, the chapters in the following pages will deal about the wastelands and unit cost of fuelwood production of various species under different agro-climatic regions of the country.

2

GENESIS OF ENERGY FORESTRY

It takes a long time to change the traditional rural life to a state where modern parameters of living are observed. The social and economic changes are sometimes not well adopted during a span of the generation. The changing results of economic activities in a short period are more positive-oriented than the social ones. In such a subsistence economy, people are more dependent on the local raw material to fulfil their necessities. The fact can be observed that in any village in India, there is heavy dependence of an average villager on bio-mass for food, fodder, fuel, fertilizers, fibre, building materiai, medicine and small cottage industrial ventures. This situation is not likely to change in the foreseable future. The increasing needs of the rural people can not be met from the natural forest stands, as it would further reduce the forest area of the country. Thus the destruction of forests will not stop as long as fuel for cooking is either not provided free to the rural poor, or is not made available very cheap.

Our objective of the planning should be that every village is able to meet its fuelwood, fodder, food and other bio-mass requirements by growing trees and shrubs on the very available piece of vacant land. And then it would be possible to raise fuelwood crops on such lands by choosing suitable species and applying correct planting techniques. In fact, the time has come when country must plan for meeting bio-mass needs from the plantations.

In order to obtain the maximum productivity of fuelwood in minimum time, high density and short rotation biomass of fast and hardy species of deciduous trees and shrubs should be grown. The productivity of fuelwood species has to be judged in terms of weight as the plants do not develop clean stems. The studies have shown that the initial expenditure on fuelwood farming is higher on wastelands than on fertile lands. The returns in economic terms are low but there are good social benefits. Experiments conducted in India and elsewhere indicate that a stage has now reached where fuelwoods can be economically farmed with inputs of selected species and varieties, labour, water, nurseries, fertilisers and pesticides.

The need to maximise of woody bio-mass has given rise to term 'Energy Forestry', the evolution of which may be treated in the following sequence; natural forests, unscientific forestry, scientific forestry, protection forestry, conservation forestry, production forestry, dynamic production forestry, social forestry, and energy forestry.

The genesis of energy forestry can be traced back to a number of phases. In the past, forests were used to be cut indiscriminately and exploited haphazardly for a variety of individual uses. These practices led to a number of changes in the micro-climate as well as soil degradation. The issue of a memorandum of the Government of India in 1855 was the first step taken towards scientific conservation, mapping and classification of forests. The formulation of the forest policy in 1894 mainly aimed at preserving the minimum area under forests and to exploit forests and commercial value as a source of revenue to the State. This policy resulted in the destruction of even every sensitive, fastest yielding, renewable, evergreen rain forests.

The creation of roads and tracts in forest tended to destroy almost the whole forest. The local population got no benefit from these transactions other than low paid temporary employment now and then. They resorted to massive illegal utilisation of fodder, feed, fertiliser, timber and fuel from the forests for their immediate needs. The National Forests Policy formulated in 1952 did not materially bring about any changes because the choice of tree species for establishing man-made forests was still biased towards industrial needs. It was only in 1971, the Government of India changed its approach from the conservation forestry to dynamic production forestry. The main objective of this policy was to bring about a shift from just producing raw materials from industries to rural development and helping the poor people to progress. These ideas led to the genesis of the concept of 'social forestry' which is regarded as an instrument of socio-economic changes in the rural community, through their active involvement for a number of activities producing food, fuel, fodder, fibre, fertilizers and timber providing protection of lands from winds, erosion, pollution and desertification; bringing about soil improvement, humidity control, water-recycling, flow regulation, sheltering of birds and insects; and creating recreational facilities. This scheme has two components:

(i) *Rural Fuelwood Plantation:* Under this programme, fast growing fuelwood species suitable to localities are planted on community lands, wastelands including coastal wastelands and degraded forests; sides of roads, canals, railway lines; and in and around individual farms, in the compounds of schools and public buildings and in the backyards of individual houses.

(ii) *Farm Forestry:* Under this programme, well grown seedlings prepared in nurseries are supplied to farmers and the children under 'A tree for every child' programme free of charge. State Forest Departments ensure timely technical guidance about site preparation, choice of species etc. through their execution wing.

In the beginning, it was proposed to cover about 100 districts (25% of the total number of districts) all over the country which are chronically deficit in fuelwood but later on to ensure a wider coverage of area, 157 districts were finally selected from all the States and four Union Territories of Arunachal Pradesh, Mizoram, Delhi and Goa, Daman and Diu.

At a time when the fuelwood accounts for nearly four-fifths of the energy needs of most of the rural families and about half the urban families in India, the fuelwood problem has assumed even greater importance after 1973. Thus social forestry concept has now taken the form of energy forestry.

An energy tree or shrub is one which is grown for the purpose of harvesting fuelwood. There are many factors that influence selection of suitable fuelwood species. Density, calorific value, growth rate, period of harvest, coppicing power, smooth burning with least smoke are some of them. In case of energy trees, important consideration is not only quick growth of trees but also its calorific value and density. The higher the density and calorific value, the better the species as fuelwood.

Dry miscellaneous forests are principal source of fuelwood yield where working system is simple coppice or its modification with 30-40 years rotation. Irrespective of very fast growing and excellent coppicing tree species, what we take out of forests is much less than its yield capacity. This requires sound planning in forest management of the region where energy trees and shrubs are to be established. Energy forestry is thus the creation, conservation, scientific management and optimal utilisation of energy trees until they are transported out of the plantation. The following are various types of energy forestry: natural firewood, commercial firewood, block plantations, non-commercial firewood block plantations farms, firewood gardens, urban green belts, and others. Commercial plantations are similar to the agricultural lands where inputs such as water, fertilizers, pesticides, human and animal labour are used to obtain maximum yield in minimum time. These have progressively been planted in almost all the States of the country.

Review of Performance and Targets

Various agencies are involved in the afforestation programme in the country. There are external aided projects too in a number of States. The combined progress report indicate that the target for total afforestation was 343 crore seedlings. Of this, 344 crore seedlings had been achieved by 31st January, 1987. This means an achievement of 100 per cent. The targets have been exceeded by Assam, Bihar, Gujarat, Kerala, M.P., Meghalaya, Nagaland, Rajasthan and U.P. Andhra Pradesh, Haryana, Karnataka, Maharashtra, Manipur, Orissa, Punjab, Sikkim, Tripura and West Bengal have fallen slightly short of the targets. The remaining States have performed considerably below the targets (see Annexures 2.1 to 2.18).

The proposed targets under different programmes and agencies for the remaining period of the Seventh Five Year Plan have also been given in annexures. The NWDB report suggests that the target of 5 million hectares per year of afforestation would mean 10 billion saplings. Assuming a cost of 50 paise to raise one sapling and Rs. 2.00 for its plantation (inclusive of ground preparation, digging pits, fertilizer, weeding, watering, protection etc.) the funds required for raising saplings would be of the order of Rs. 500 crores a year and for plantation Rs. 2,000 crores per year. In other words, the cost of afforesting 5 million hectares per year would mean Rs. 2,500 crores (per ha/2000 trees/Rs. 5,000).

The latest available information indicates that an area of more than seven million hectares has been brought under afforestation during the first four years of the Seventh Plan. Of them more than two million hectares have been afforested during 1988-89 itself till December 1988. In 1987-88, a total of 1.8 million hectares were afforested.

The rate of diversion of forest land for non-forest purposes come down to 15,000 hectares a year during 1987-88 from 1.5 lakh hectares before 1980, when the Forest Conservation Act was enacted.

The forest cover in almost all the States except Haryana, Himachal

Pradesh, Jammu and Kashmir, Punjab and Tripura had gone up in recent years. The total forest cover had gone up to 6,42,040 sq.km in 1981-83 from 5,55,180 sq.km in 1972-75. The 1972-75 figure is based on the National Remote Sensing Agency whereas the 1981-83 figure is based on reconciled figures of the Forest Survey of India. The forest cover has come down in all the metropolitan cities because of increased construction activities.

The afforestation target for 1988-89 is 1.28 million hectares. The area brought under afforestation during the first three years of Seventh Plan had been 1.5 million hectares in 1985-86, 1.76 million hectares in 1986-87 and 1.8 million hectares in 1987-88. The target set for 1989-90 is 2.5 million hectares.

Thus the area brought under afforestation is increasing year after year and Plan after Plan. The area afforested during the first three years of the Seventh Plan itself was more than the total area brought under afforestation during the first 30 years i.e. between 1950 and 1980. It was also more than the total area brought under afforestation during the Sixth Plan period.

An area of 4.65 million hectares was brought under afforestation during the Sixth Plan as against 3.5 million hectare between 1950 and 1980. An average of 0.93 million hectares was brought under afforestation per year during the Sixth Plan period as against an average of 0.11 million hectares a year prior to 1980.

Apart from cost factor and physical achievements, the coordination of different agencies to implement the programme at the field level is a major task. Since the programme is a time bound and growing of saplings and establishment of plantation can not be taken up the year round, there is necessity of monitoring of the programme at every step for all the States/Union Territories.

ANNEXURE 2.1

Prosperity Through Social Forestry

BIOMASS					
Fuel	Food	Fodder	Rural cottage industries	Employment	Environment
* Easier availability of fuel	* Supplementary food for tribal and other people	* Easy availability of nutritious fodder	* Regular supply of tree-based raw material	* Generates employment	* Rational land use
* Cheaper substitute for commercial fuel	* Availability of fruits, protein-rich seeds, flowers at low cost	* Diversion of land to food production	* Growth of chain of rural cottage industries	* Check on the migration of rural population to towns	* Optimization of use of renewable resources
* Release of cow-dung for manure	* Improvement in health of rural living	* Improvement in cattle wealth	* Development of co-operative societies and rural financing agencies	* Job opportunities for landless	* Development of water resources
* Lesser pressure on Govt. forests	* Growth of subsidiary fruit-based industries	* Improvement in human health		* Multifarious economic activities	* Conservation of soil
* Renewable resources of energy	* Help in solving national food crisis	* Improvement in soil fertility through more manure	* Raising of socio-economic status	* Additional income to the village population	* Bio-aesthetic development
* Improvement of soil fertility				* Rise in rural per capita income	* Better health
					* Creation of oxygen bank
					* Control of water, air, noise, pollutions.

Source: O.P. Vimal and P.D. Tyagi (1985).

ANNEXURE 2.2

List of 157 Districts Selected for Implementation of the New Centrally-sponsored Scheme 'Social Forestry including Rural Fuelwood Plantation'

1. Andhra Pradesh

    1) Rangareddy
    2) Guntur
    3) Medak
    4) Nalgonda
    5) Krishna
    6) Nellore
    7) Prakasam
    8) Nizamabad

2. Assam

    1) Kamrup
    2) Goalpara
    3) Sibsagar
    4) Cachar

3. Bihar

    1) Santhal Parganas
    2) Bhagalpur
    3) Giridh
    4) Dhanbad
    5) Hazaribagh
    6) Gaya
    7) Aurangabad
    8) Nalanda
    9) Monghyr
    10) Rohtas

4. Gujarat

    1) Vadodara
    2) Panchmahal
    3) Kutch
    4) Surindranagar
    5) Sabarkantha
    6) Jamnagar
    7) Bhavnagar

5. Haryana

    1) Karnal
    2) Mahendragarh
    3) Kurukshetra
    4) Gurgaon
    5) Sonepat

6. Himachal Pradesh

    1) Kangra
    2) Mandi
    3) Sirmur
    4) Simla
    5) Hamirpur

7. Jammu & Kashmir

    1) Anantnag
    2) Rajouri
    3) Kargil
    4) Kathua

8. Karnataka

    1) Bangalore
    2) Gulbarga
    3) Kolar
    4) Bellary
    5) Mandya
    6) Dharwad
    7) Mysore
    8) Chickmagalur

9. Kerala

    1) Cannanore

2) Trivandrum
3) Kozhikode
4) Kottayam

10.Madhya Pradesh

1) Rewa
2) Ratlam
3) Indore
4) Bhopal
5) Gwalior
6) Jhabua
7) Seony
8) Jabalpur
9) Bilaspur
10) Raipur
11) Satna
12) Durg
13) Sagar
14) Khandwa
15) Panna

11.Maharashtra

1) Ahmednagar
2) Tarnagiri
3) Sholapur
4) Usmanabad
5) Kolhapur
6) Parbhani
7) Nasik
8) Pune
9) Thane
10) Jalgaon

12.Manipur

1) Manipur Central
2) Manipur North

13.Meghalaya

1) West Khashi Hills
2) West Garo Hills

14.Nagaland

1) Kohima
2) Phek
3) Tuensang

15. Orissa

1) Balasore
2) Cuttack
3) Bolangir
4) Puri
5) Ganjam

16. Punjab

1) Amritsar
2) Patiala
3) Ferozepur
4) Gurdaspur
5) Faridkot

17. Rajasthan

1) Jaipur
2) Udaipur
3) Bharatpur
4) Alwar
5) Bhilwara
6) Ajmer
7) Banswara
8) Jhunjhunu
9) Kota
10) Swaimadhopur

18. Sikkim

1) East Gangtok
2) South Gangtok

19. Tamil Nadu

1) Madurai
2) Trichirappalli
3) Chengalpattu
4) Dharampuri
5) North Arcot
6) South Arcot

20. Tripura

1) West District
2) North District

21. Uttar Pradesh

1) Hamirpur
2) Jalaun
3) Pilibhit
4) Kheri
5) Jhansi
6) Lalitpur
7) Tehri
8) Almora
9) Garhwal
10) Mirzapur
11) Meerut
12) Allahabad
13) Deoria
14) Gorakhpur
15) Jaunpur
16) Azamgarh
17) Moradabad
18) Agra
19) Aligarh

22. West Bengal

1) Burdwan
2) Midnapore
3) Bankura
4) 24-Parganas
5) Birbhum
6) Nadia

Union Territories

1. Arunachal Pradesh

1) West Kameng
2) Lower Subansiri
3) Dibang Valley
4) Tirap
5) Lohit
6) East Kameng
7) Upper Subansiri
8) East Siang
9) West Siang

2. Delhi

1) Delhi

3. Mizoram

1) Aizwal
2) Lungloi
3) Hintuipuri

4. Goa, Daman & Diu

1) Goa

Source: Govt. of India, Ministry of Agriculture, Social Forestry (1984).

ANNEXURE 2.3

Gravity and Calorific Value of Wood of Some Tree Species

Species	Per cent moisture in green condition	Specific Gravity in green condition	Specific Gravity at 12% moisture content	Calorific values of dried material (calories/gm)
Acacia catechu	33.6	1.169	1.005	S 5142 H 5244
Acacia chundra	29.3	1.262	1.120	
Acacia leucophloea	53.5	1.013	0.786	S 4899
Aegle marmelos	41.2	1.065	0.907	S 4886 4495
Albizia lebbeck	73.6	0.953	0.640	S 5163 H 5166
A. odoratissima	87.9	1.188	0.735	S 5131 H 5266
Albizia procera	96.2	1.136	0.682	S 4870 H 4865
Casuarina equifolia	36.7	0.947	0.854	4950
Dalbargia sisso	54.3-69.7	1.068- 1.091	0.803- 0.748	S 4908 H 5180
Syzgium cumini	70.5	1.103	0.782	4834
Gmelina arborea	144.5- 151.2	1.088- 1.053	0.518- 0.486	4763
Holoptelea intergrifolia	81.9	0.906	0.586	5258
Mallotus philippinesis	76.3	1.007	0.678	4835
Azadirachta indica	56.7	1.086	0.819	
Prosopis spicigera	61.7	1.025	0.763	5003
Terminalia arjuna	73.3	1.189	0.819	S 5030 H 5128
Terminalia belerica	46.7	1.000	0.813	4972
Terminalia chebula	51.2	1.169	0.947	3967
Terminalia alata	53.5-66.5	1.085- 1.151	0.842 0.833	S 5047 H 5373

S — sapwood; H — heartwood.

Source: M.M. Pant (1981).

ANNEXURE 2.4

Selected Energy Trees

Species	Wood density	Calorific value (cal/ gm)	Diameter at breast height (cm)	Age at harvest for fuelwood (yrs)
		Plantations		
Acacia nilotica	0.806	4946	12.0	15
Anthocephalus chinensis	0.498	4800	18.5	20
Dalbergia sissoo	0.779	5180	12.9	15
Eucalyptus grandis	0.700 (estimated)	4900 (approx)	19.4	13.5
Eucalyptus tereticornis (plantation)	0.700	4800	7.0	6
Eucalpytus tereticornis (coppice)	0.700	4800	9.9	14
Tectona grandis	0.664	5535	9.4	15
		Coppic Crops		
Acacia catechu	1.005	5244	13.5	30
Amogeissus latifolia	0.935	4909	12.1	30
Diospyros melanosylon	0.826	5030	12.8	30
Aegle marmoelos	0.907	4495	10.7	30
Largerstroemia parviflora	0.749	4885	12.7	30
Lamnea coromandelica	0.584	4933	13.2	30
Madhuca latifolia	0.915	5224	10.7	30
Qugenia oojeinensis	0.846	5178	10.0	30
Pterocarpus marsupium	0.796	5141	14.9	30
Quercus robusta	0.878	5433	17.8	30
		Natural Forests		
Anogessus pendula	0.946	4739	8.5	30
Boswellia serrata	0.580	5169	13.8	30
Ceous deodara	0.548	5076	42.7	80
Pinus excelsa	0.507	4995	46.2	90
Pinus roxburghii	0.541	4961	41.4	80
Quercus spp.	0.948	4633	16.8	30
Shorea robusta	0.878	5433	26.4	85

Source: O.P. Vimal & P.D. Tyagi (1986).

ANNEXURE 2.5

Forest Cover of India

Category	NRSA's estimate 1980-82		FSI's estimate 1981-83		Reconcilled Corrected (partly upto 1984)	
	Area (sq.km)	%	Area (sq.km)	%	Area (sq.km)	%
1	2	3 @	4	5 @	6	7 @
1. Closed forest	360229 *	10.96	360046	10.9**	357686	10.88*
2. Open forest	100592 $	3.06	282026	8.60$$	276583	8.41$$
3. Mangrove forest	2649	0.081	4247	0.10	4046	0.12
4. Coffee Plantations	—	—	2376	0.10	3726	0.11
Total***	463470	14.10	648695	19.7	642041	19.52

@ Expressed as per cent of the geographical area of the country
* Crown cover 30 per cent or more
** Crown cover 40 per cent or more
$ Crown cover 10-30 per cent
$$ Crown cover 10-40 per cent
*** Scrub areas with less than 10 per cent crown cover have not been included.

ANNEXURE 2.6

Fuelwood Species and Conditions of their Growth

Species	Annual Rainfall (in)	Annual Rainfall (mm)	Soil condition	Growth vigor
Acacia arabica	3–50	76–1270	Alluvial	Very fast
A. catechu	20–100	508–2540	Alluvial	Very fast
Acacia spp. other indigenous	20–100	508–2540	Alluvial	Moderate
Albizzia proceera and A. lebbeck	30–80	762–2032	All soils	Moderate
Azadirachta indica	20–45	508–1143	All soils	Fast
Cassia sismea	20–100	worked up 508–2540 including laterite	Any soils	Moderate
Casuarina equisetifolia	*30–150*	*762–3810*	*Coastal, Sandy*	*Very fast*
Dalbergia sissoo	30–100	762–2540 including laterite	Any soil,	Fast
Eucalyptus globules	50–100	1270–2540	Fairly deep	Very fast
Eucalyptus spp. other	20–80	508–2032	Any soil	Moderate
Eugenia jambolana	30–100	762–2540 soil	Any moist	Moderate
Macaranga denticulate	50–100	1270–2540 loamy	Fairly deep,	Very fast
Morua alba and M. Indica	20–80	508–2032	Fairly deep, loamy	Very fast
Prosopia juliflora	10–50	254–1270	Any soil	Fast
P.spicigera	20–35	508–889	Any soil	Moderate
Quercus spp.	80–120	2032–3048 hills	Fairly deep,	Moderate
Shorea robusta	30–100	762–2540 including laterite	Any soil,	Moderate
Terminallia spp.	20–100	508–2540 including laterite	Any soil,	Moderate
Zizyphus jujuba	5–80	127–2032 including laterite	Any soil,	Moderate

Source: S.P. W.D. (1984).

ANNEXURE 2.7

Statewise Forest Area and Forest Growing Stock

State/Union Territory	Geographical area ('000 ha)	Forest area ('000 ha)	Percentage of forest area to geographical area	Per capita forest area (hectares)	Growing stock ('000 m)
A. *States*					
Andhra Pradesh	27682	6357.1	22.96	0.119	165,355
Assam	7852	3070.8	39.11	0.154	100,000
Bihar	17388	2923.2	13.36	0.042	71,068
Gujarat	19598	1964.8	10.02	0.058	14,347
Haryana	4422	169.7	3.84	0.013	360
Himachal Pradesh	5567	2114.2	37.97	0.499	81,250
Jammu & Kashmir	22224	2188.6	9.85	0.366	98,113
Karnataka	19177	3838.6	20.01	0.103	53,227
Kerala	3887	1125.1	28.94	0.044	201,556
Madhya Pradesh	44284	15541.4	35.09	0.298	600,000
Maharashtra	30776	6416.7	20.85	0.102	73,471
Manipur	2236	1515.4	67.77	1.056	72,411
Meghalaya	2249	851.0	37.84	0.640	*
Nagaland	1653	289.9	17.53	0.375	1,911
Orissa	15578	5996.3	38.49	0.228	109,000
Punjab	5036	259.2	12.73	0.015	879
Rajasthan	34221	3043.9	8.89	0.089	3,000
Sikkim	730	282.0	38.63	0.892	N.A.
Tamil Nadu	13007	2201.4	16.92	0.045	4,000
Uttar Pradesh	29441	5114.9	17.37	0.046	96,157
West Bengal	8785	1183.0	13.46	0.021	16,000
B. *Union Territories*					
Andaman & Nicobar Islands	829	714.4	86.17	3,800	71,000
Arunachal Pradesh	8358	5154.0	61.66	8,207	117,000
Dadra and Nagar Haveli	49	20.2	41.22	0.191	N.A.
Delhi	149	Negligible	—	—	N.A.
Goa, Daman & Diu	381	130.9	34.35	0.121	3,000
Mizoram	2109	1662.9	78.84	3.407	674
Other Union Territories	63	—	—	—	—
All India:	328,779	74721.6	22.73	0.109	1,964,416

N.A. Not Available   * Included under Assam.

Source: (i) India's forests — 1980 and 1984 Central Forestry Commission, New Delhi.
(ii) Development of forestry and forest products-country profile-India, Govt. of India, Ministry of Agriculture 1981.

ANNEXURE 2.8

Social Forestry Projects in India – Anticipated Physical Targets (1982–87) (ha)

State	Agency	Total cost (Rs. mill)	Village woodlots	Farm forestry	Institutional lands	Community self help	Canal	Readsides Railway	Railway	Degraded forests	Total
U.P.	World Bank	400	5,000	4,000	—	3,080	16,000	7,000	4,000	13,600	52,680
Gujarat	World Bank	654	37,400	76,000	—	—	2,000	31,600	3,400	30,000	1,80,400
W.B.	World Bank	349	6,000	52,000	—	—	—	20,000	—	15,000	93,000
Haryana	World Bank	316	12,000	21,780	1,000	—	4,850	3,200	800	15,500	59,130
J&K	World Bank	237	15,500	3,000	1,270	—	—	—	—	17,000	3,770
Karnataka	World Bank	592	8,000 @	10,000	—	—	2,000	18,000	—	60,000	1,88,000
Tamil Nadu	Sida	450	1,32,000 @	39,200	—	5,250 (fodder)	—	6,075 km	—	—	1,62,300
Bihar	Sida	400	—	20,000	—	3,500 (tasser)	—	—	—	72,000	95,500
Orissa	Sida	230	25,000	1,387	—	—	—	—	—	37,000	73,195
Maharashtra	USAID	564	5,250	2,750	—	—	—	28,195	—	37,000	73,195
M.P.	USAID	470	48,000	—	—	—	—	15,450	—	—	63,450
A.P.	CIDA	400	47,000 @	1,02,000	—	—	—	—	—	42,000	1,91,000
Total		5,062	3,41,150	4,07,967	2,270	11,830	24,850	1,23,445	8,200	3,37,180	12,56,812 + 6,075 km

@ Tank foreshore.

Note: Village woodlots are on community lands. Farm Forestry is on private lands.

ANNEXURE 2.9

State-wise Details of Area under Forest Cover (1981-83) as assessed by the Forest Survey of India

Name of State/UT	Geographical area (km^2)	Forest cover (km^2)	Percentage area under forest cover to geographical area
1. Andhra Pradesh	276820	50194	18.13
2. Arunachal Pradesh	83580	60500	72.38
3. Assam	78580	26386	33.57
4. Bihar	173880	28748	16.53
5. Goa (including) Daman & Diu)	3810	1285	33.72
6. Gujarat	195980	13570	6.92
7. Haryana	44220	644	1.46
8. Himachal Pradesh	55670	12882	23.14
9. Jammu & Kashmir	222240	20880	9.39
10. Karnataka	191770	32264	16.82
11. Kerala	38870	10402	26.76
12. Madhya Pradesh	442840	127749	28.85
13. Maharashtra	307760	47416	15.41
14. Manipur	22360	17679	79.06
15. Meghalaya	22490	16511	73.41
16. Mizoram	21090	19092	90.52
17. Nagaland	16530	14351	86.82
18. Orissa	155780	53163	34.13
19. Punjab	50360	766	1.52
20. Rajasthan	342210	12478	3.64
21. Sikkim	7300	2839	38.89
22. Tamil Nadu	130070	18380	14.13
23. Tripura	10480	5743	54.79
24. Uttar Pradesh	294411	31443	10.67
25. West Bengal	87850	8811	10.03
26. A & N Islands	8290	7603	91.71
27. Chandigarh	114	2	1.75
28. Dadra & Nagar Haveli	490	237	48.36
29. Delhi	1490	15	1.01
30. Lakshadweep	30	—	—
31. Pondicherry	492	8	1.62
TOTAL	3287797	642041	
Percentage of geographical area		19.52%	

ANNEXURE 2.10

Change in Forest Cover in India

State/Union Territory	Total forest area, sq.km 1972-75	1980-82	Change in forest area sq. km.
Andhra Pradesh	49049	40435	(-) 8614
Assam	21055	19796	(-) 1259
Bihar	22687	20139	(-) 2548
Gujarat	9459	5057	(-) 4402
Haryana	757	401	(-) 356
Himachal Pradesh	15075	9130	(-) 5945
Jammu & Kashmir	22335	14361	(-) 7974
Karnataka	29480	25655	(-) 3825
Kerala	8611	7376	(-) 1235
Madhya Pradesh	108568	90215	(-) 18353
Maharashtra	40682	30350	(-) 10332
Manipur	15090	13572	(-) 1518
Meghalaya	14390	12458	(-) 1932
Nagaland	8154	8095	(-) 59
Tripura	6330	5138	(-) 1192
Orissa	48383	39425	(-) 8958
Punjab & Chandigarh	1120	499	(-) 621
Rajasthan	11294	5972	(-) 5322
Tamil Nadu	16676	13187	(-) 3489
Uttar Pradesh	25869	21022	(-) 4847
West Bengal	8347	6483	(+) 1864
Sikkim	1761	2883	(+) 1122
Arunachal Pradesh	51438	58104	(+) 666
Delhi	18	10	(-) 8
Mizoram	13860	11971	(-) 1889
TOTAL	551709	448305	(-) 103404

Source: The National Remote Sensing Agency (NSRA), Hyderabad.

ANNEXURE 2.11

Proposed Targets for Different Programmes and Agencies, 1987-90

(in million ha)

Social Forestry	1987-88	1988-89	1989-90
(i) Farm Forestry	1.50	2.00	3.00
(ii) Block plantations on Govt. & Community Land	0.75	0.75	0.75
(iii) Degraded Forest Land	0.50	1.00	1.50
Forest Dev. Corporation	0.10	0.15	0.20
Land Development Banks	0.12	0.18	0.25
Industry:			
Forest based			
Oil-bearing Trees			
Others			
Cooperative & Voluntary Agencies	0.10	0.20	0.30
Afforestation of Mined Areas	0.10	0.20	0.30
P.S.Us.	0.02	0.02	0.02
Railways	0.02	0.02	0.02
Highways	0.01	0.01	0.01
Aerial Seeding	0.05	0.07	0.10
Total	3.32	4.67	6.55

Source: NWDB.

ANNEXURE 2.12

Targets and Achievements, 1986-87

Sl. No.	State	Seedlings in lakhs		Targets for Afforestation 1987-88		
		Target 1986-87	Achievements upto Jan.1987	Farm Forestry (Seedlings in lakhs)	Block Plantations (ha)	Total Afforestation (Seedlings in lakhs)
1.	Andhra Pradesh	3000	2747	2520	54000	3600
2.	Assam	400	625	490	10500	700
3.	Bihar	2600	2711	2450	52500	3500
4.	Gujarat	1631	2271	1750	37500	2500
5.	Haryana	725	644	507	10900	725
6.	Himachal Pradesh	625	567	630	13500	900
7.	Jammu & Kashmir	522	244	490	10500	700
8.	Karnataka	2500	2279	2240	48000	3200
9.	Kerala	1200	1519	1260	27000	1800
10.	Madhya Pradesh	3700	3920	3500	75000	5000
11.	Maharashtra	2400	2352	2240	48000	3200
12.	Manipur	160	144	140	3000	200
13.	Meghalaya	150	158	140	3000	200
14.	Nagaland	350	403	420	9000	600
15.	Orissa	2400	2161	2240	48000	3200
16.	Punjab	550	502	525	11250	750
17.	Rajasthan	1100	1315	1120	24000	1600
18.	Sikkim	110	114	105	2250	150
19.	Tamil Nadu	2400	1711	2240	48000	3200
20.	Tripura	320	268	280	6000	400
21.	Uttar Pradesh	4500	4865	4200	9000	6000
22.	West Bengal	1400	1365	1260	27000	1800
23.	A & N Islands	120	116	91	1950	130
24.	Arunachal Pradesh	125	26	87.5	1875	125
25.	Chandigarh	3.40	3.6	3.575	5	
26.	Delhi	50	44	44.8	960	64
27.	Dadra & Nagar Haveli	30	31	28	600	40
28.	Goa, Daman & Diu	75	68	70	1500	100
29.	Lakshadweep	0.12	0.27	0.21	4.5	0.30
30.	Mizoram	1128	1281	1120	21000	1600
31.	Pondicherry	10	8.93	7.49	160.5	10.70
	Total	34284.52	34460.80	32199.5	690025	46000

Source: NWDB.

ANNEXURE 2.13

Centrally-sponsored Scheme Rural Fuelwood Plantation and Afforestation of Eco-sensitive Non Himalayan Areas (1986-87)

Sl. No.	Name of State/UT	Financial (Rs. in lakh)				Physical progress			
						Target		Achievement	
		Allocation	Admissibility	Amount released	Expenditure	Plantation (in ha.)	Distribution of seedling (in lakh no.)	Plantation (in ha.)	Distribution of seedling (in lakh no.)
(1)	(2)	(3)	(4)	(5)	(6)	(7)	(8)	(9)	(10)
1.	Andhra Pradesh	120.00	120.00	85.00	131.89	5600	404.40	3159	118.60
2.	Assam	120.00	111.68	102.00	87.35	5200	175.00	5200	76.10
3.	Bihar	167.00	167.00	114.00	251.02	9600	150.00	9600	150.00
4.	Gujarat	120.00	75.51	52.00	64.63	2500	25.00	2594	25.00
5.	Haryana	60.00	60.00	35.00	84.97	2500	—	1906	—
6.	Himachal Pradesh	80.00	95.04	24.00	126.94	3960	—	2675	—
7.	Jammu & Kashmir	40.00	22.00	15.00	13.53	1115	27.80	510	10.40
8.	Karnataka	110.00	102.27	74.00	64.37	1137	143.75	1137	120.00
9.	Kerala	90.00	90.00	NIL	8.15	4000	—	7	55.56
10.	Madhya Pradesh	178.00	74.00	NIL	112.90	5925	300.00	5985	42.84

(Contd.)

ANNEXURE — 2.13 (*Contd.*)

(1)	(2)	(3)	(4)	(5)	(6)	(7)	(8)	(9)	(10)
11.	Maharashtra	54.00	41.57	27.00	16.58	3800	—	NR	—
12.	Manipur	50.00	45.50	38.00	50.16	2750	—	2755	—
13.	Meghalaya	50.00	47.74	35.00	11.46	1540	24.00	1540	14.97
14.	Nagaland	80.00	72.00	66.00	54.00	6770	30.00	6770	18.00
15.	Orissa	120.00	133.00	85.00	221.20	9860	15.00	9221	15.00
16.	Punjab	90.00	135.74	64.00	200.16	5000	150.00	4657	101.60
17.	Rajasthan	130.00	110.00	80.00	141.20	6000	75.00	6000	75.00
18.	Sikkim	30.00	18.55	NIL	39.50	700	7.00	750	7.00
19.	Tamil Nadu	96.00	64.26	NIL	44.68	3500	153.00	1025	126.09
20.	Tripura	50.00	37.50	35.00	64.14	3000	30.00	2740	48.93
21.	Uttar Pradesh	170.00	142.07	80.00	166.32	4600	223.00	4539	223.00
22.	West Bengal	40.00	25.00	NIL	2.92	—	15.50	—	15.50
Union Territories									
23.	Arunachal Pradesh	25.00	6.47	5.00	1.49	195	1.30	90	—
24.	Delhi	20.00	18.98	8.00	8.00	415	4.00	365	1.99
25.	Goa. Daman & Diu	20.00	17.08	10.00	NR	500	20.00	600	—
26.	Mizoram	100.00	118.59	70.00	86.13	3797	10.00	3797	10.00
	Total	2210.00	1951.45	1104.00	2053.69	9364	1983.75	77622	1255.58

* N.R. Not reported.

Source: NWDB.

ANNEXURE 2.14

Centrally-sponsored Scheme, Soil, Water, Tree Conservation in Himalayas Operation Soil Watch 1986-87

Sl. No.	Name of State/ UT	Financial				Physical Progress	
		Allocation (Rs. in lakh)	Addmissibility (Rs. in lakh	Amount released (Rs. in lakh	Expenditure (Rs. in lakh)	Target	Achievement
						Area to be treated (in ha)	Area achieved (in ha)
1.	Assam	30.00	30.00	15.00	7.16	798	650
2.	Haryana	116.00	120.00	119.16	77.70	3000	3191
3.	Himachal Pradesh	210.00	203.64	105.00	83.62	5250	2628
4.	Jammu & Kashmir	40.00	39.60	20.00	5.80	1003	3.40
5.	Manipur	40.00	40.00	39.20	18.36	2255	3460
6.	Meghalaya	80.00	74.18	40.00	NR	5587	NR
7.	Nagaland	90.00	103.00	45.00	NR	11548	NR
8.	Punjab	50.00	121.65	121.56	52.96	3750	3750
9.	Sikkim	34.00	45.00	17.00	26.72	1457	571
10.	Tripura	36.00	31.70	20.00	17.33	1000	1242
11.	U.P.	164.00	163.14	82.00	104.90	4100	4151
12.	W.B.	70.00	69.43	35.00	40.93	2221	2039
13.	Arunachal Pradesh	18.00	3.79	0.06	0.06	226	60
14.	Mizoram	100.00	112.00	112.00	70.19	4011	38.11
		1078.00	1157.89	777.02	505.73	46206	25556.40

N.R. — Not Reported.
Source: NWDB.

ANNEXURE 2.15

Centrally-sponsored Scheme ..... Decentralised People's Nurseries

Sl. No.	Name of State/ UT	Rs. in lakhs				Seedlings in crores	
		Allocation	Admissibility	Released	Expenditure	Physical Target	Progress achieved
1.	Andhra Pradesh	10.00	10.00	10.00	NR	0.22	NR
2.	Assam	10.00	10.00	10.00	"	0.22	"
3.	Gujarat	200.00	200.00	200.00	"	4.44	"
4.	Haryana	55.50	55.50	55.50	"	1.23	"
5.	Himachal Pradesh	20.00	20.00	20.00	"	0.44	"
6.	Kerala	43.50	43.50	43.50	"	0.96	"
8.	Madhya Pradesh	100.00	100.00	50.00*	"	2.21	"
9.	Maharashtra	27.00	27.00	27.00	"	0.60	"
10.	Manipur	10.00	10.00	10.00	"	0.22	"
11.	Meghalaya	10.00	10.00	10.00	"	0.22	"
12.	Nagaland	10.00	10.00	10.00	"	0.22	"
13.	Orissa	60.00	60.00	60.00	"	1.33	"
14.	Punjab	40.00	40.00	40.00	"	0.88	"
15.	Rajasthan	30.00	30.00	30.00	"	0.66	"
16.	Tamil Nadu	20.00	20.00	20.00	"	0.44	"
17.	Tripura	10.00	10.00	10.00	"	0.22	"
18.	West Bengal	38.00	38.00	38.00	"	0.64	"
19.	Delhi	2.00	2.00	2.00	"	0.44	"
20.	Mizoram	10.00	10.00	10.00	"	0.22	"
	Total	726.00	726.00	676.00	"	16.13	"
	NDDB	124.29	124.29	124.29	"	2.76	"
	G.Total	850.29	850.29	850.29	"	18.89	"

* In the case of MP 2nd Instalment of Rs. 50.00 lakh is due to be released soon?

* Rs. 0.29 lakhs to be reappropriated from other Scheme.

Source: NWDB.

ANNEXURE 2.16

Afforestation Through Earmarked Funds Under NREP and REEGP Schemes

State/UT	Rs. Lakhs				Physical Achievements			
	Allocation	Expenditure	Allocation	Expenditure	Area (ha)		Trees Planted (Lacks)	
	NREP	NREP	RLEGP	RLEGP	NREP	RLEGP	NREP	RLEGP
1	2	3	4	5	6	7	8	9
Andhra Pradesh	1098.50	735.10 66.92%	887.25	474.61 53.49%	11,288	12,214	301	51.00
Assam	230.50	55.01	185.25	40.00 21.59%	973			
Bihar	1617.00	—	1305.75	1098.00 84.09%				
Gujarat	378.50	274.44 72.50%	305.75	227.36 74.36%	6,762	4,804	180	
Haryana	107.00		86.50	43.78 50.61%	1,592			17.51
Himachal Pradesh	69.00		57.75	16.50 28.57%	1,208	1,045		8.80
Jammu & Kashmir	85.00		70.00	4.92 7.03%				
Karnataka	530.00	350.00 66.04%	429.50	286.00 66.59%	7,700	5,359		
Kerala	433.00	307.82 71.09%	348.50	220.47 63.26%		588		30.20
M.P.	953.50		770.25	591.17 76.75%				
Maharashtra	917.00	350.84 38.26%	739.50	163.63 22.13%	4110	16,082	351	
Manipur	12.50	19.15 153.20%	10.75	7.50 69.76%				
Meghalaya	17.50		13.50					
Nagaland	14.00		11.50	9.10 79.13%				
Orissa	506.50	342.34 67.59%	409.75	203.71 49.72%	22,576	38,366	222	

(*Contd.*)

ANNEXURE — 2.16 (*Contd.*)

1	2	3	4	5	6	7	8	9
Punjab	114.00		92.00	49.78 54.11%		965		19
Rajasthan	446.00	305.21 68.43%	363.21	314.46 86.50%	23,855	25,980		
Sikkim	9.00	8.95 99.44%	7.75	1.61 20.77%				
Tamil Nadu	905.50	620.73 68.55%	730.75	577.22 79.00%	25,909		205	
Tripura	38.00	24.48 64.42%	31.50	17.20 54.60%	1,324	1,026	34	2
U.P.	2027.00	1260.20 62.17%	1636.50	165.00 10.08%	32,605	50	75	
W.Bengal	866.00	525.15 60.64%	699.50	244.19 34.90%	4,236		27	
A&N Islands	9.00		8.00					
Arunachal Pradesh	9.00	3.52 39.11%	8.00	0.80 10.00%				
Chandigarh	2.50	2.00 80.80%	1.75					
D&N Haveli	4.00	1.24 31.00%	4.00	0.38 9.50%				
Delhi	4.50	3.00 66.67%	5.75	3.75 65.21%			1.3	1.86
Goa;Daman & Diu	10.50	6.20 59.05%	12.00	9.60 80.00%	338	300	20	30
Lakshadweep	2.50	2.84 113.40	1.75	4.67 266.86%	7km	42km		
Mizoram	9.00		8.00	3.84 48.00%				
Pondicherry	9.00	2.62 29.11%	8.00	2.70 33.75%				

Source: NWDB.

ANNEXURE 2.17

Externality Aided Social Forestry Projects in India

Sl. No.	Project Title	Project Period	Total cost of project (Rs.million)	World Bank Share	Project planting target (ha)	Achievement as on 30.9.88	
						Financial (Rs.m.)	Physical (ha)
1	2	3	4	5	6	7	8
I.	*Multilateral:*						
1.	U.P. Social Forestry Project (Phase II)	5 years (1985-86 to 1989-90	1611.6	730.8	161,950	772.61	1,60,791
2.	Gujarat Social Forestry Project (Phase-II)	5 years (1985-86 to 1989-90	1296.5	740.5	313,400	628.19	2,44,120
3.	H.P. Social Forestry Project	5 years (1985-86 to 1989-90	572.9	291.7	112,833	281.90 (up to 6/88)	56,546 (up to 6/88)
4.	Rajasthan Social Forestry Project	5 years (1985-86 to 1989-90	391.9	199.2	120,800	183.07	54,537
5.	Haryana Social Forestry Project	5 years (1982-83 to 1986-87) Extn	333.3	143.6	67,000 +15,655	335.88	76,655
6.	J & K Social Forestry Project	5 years (1982-83 to 1986-87) Extn	237.4	102.9	44,000 +12,310	294.97	59,391
7.	Karnataka Social Forestry Project	5 years (1983-84 to 1987-88	552.3	263.5	149,500	399.95 (up to 6/88)	2,96,930 (up to 6/88)
8.	Kerala Social Forestry Project	6 years (1984-85 to 1989-90)	599.1	349.8	85,300	277.57	80.971
9.	West Bengal Social Forestry Project	6 years 1981-82 to 1986-87) Extn.	348.7	232.0	93,000 +24,150	321.68 (up to 31.3.88)	1,18,008 (up to 31.3.88)

(*Contd.*)

ANNEXURE — 2.17 (*Contd.*)

1	2	3	4	5	6	7	8
II.	*Bilateral:*						
10.	A.P. Social Forestry Project (Extn.)	5 years 1983-84 to 1987-88 extended up to 1989-90	383.78	50 C M.	1,50,725	249.31	99,497
11.	Maharashtra Social Forestry Project	8 years 1982-83 to 1989-90	564.00	60 US M	81,000	450.89 (up to 6/88)	75,691 (up to 6/88)
12.	Orissa Social Forestry Project (Phase-II)	5 years 1988-89 to 1992-93	783.45	243.74 SEK M	1,34,400	47.20	21,689
13.	Bihar Social Forestry Project	6 years 1985-86 to 1990-91	538.55	206.67	1,112,268	135.57 (up to 6/88)	34,922 (up to 6/88)
14.	Tamil Nadu Social Forestry Project (Phase-II)	5 years 1988-89 to	854.00	313.00	78,380	67.13	4,200
	Grand Total :		9067.48	—	17,56,671	4445.92	13,13,948

ANNEXURE 2.18

Necessary and Presently Effected Afforestation for Fuelwood Production in Developing countries

Country	Necessary rate of affo-restation 1000 ha/yr	Present rate of affores-tation 1000 ha/yr	Afforesta-tion area needed in year 2000 1000 ha	Area Presumably afforested in the year 2000	
				1000 ha	% needed
India	250	20.0	4,000	400	10
Nigeria	100	10.0	2,000	200	10
Thailand	75	10.0	1,500	200	13
Nepal	50	5.0	1,000	100	10
Ethiopia	50	1.0	1,000	20	2
Afghanistan	50	1.0	1,000	20	2
Peru	20	5.0	400	100	25
Tanzania	20	2.5	400	50	12
Malawi	13	2.5	260	50	19
Ecuador	13	2.0	260	40	15
	640	60	11,820	1180	19

Source: Noach D & Fruhwald A. Consequence of the energy and raw material crisis for the raw material wood, in Natural Resources and Development, 16, (1982).

3

NATURE AND EXTENT OF WASTELANDS

Wastelands

The term 'wastelands' is now being used as a synonym of degraded lands. It is a general term which includes any type of land, irrespective of its ownership which is producing less than 20 per cent of its optimum biological productivity. The wastelands include degraded forests, common grazing lands, miscellaneous tree crops and groves, panchayat lands, vacant lands along railway tracks, roads and canals, fallow agricultural lands, unproductive or marginal agricultural lands and barren lands like desert, alpine area, saline and alkaline lands, ravines, eroded land etc.

There is no consensus on the definition of wastelands. There is also disagreement on various estimates of wastelands. These are at times defined as lands which are ecologically unstable or have lost top fertile soil or are having substances in soil which inhibit plant growth. These wastelands can be more precisely termed as "wasted lands" which comprise lands, the productivity of which has declined due to misuse and overuse by human and cattle population resulting into degraded ecosystems. Wastelands is better defined on the basis of the quality of the land, and the kind of land degradation problem it suffers from. Common sense indicates that wastelands produce much less than their potential. These are lands which are economically unproductive, ecologically unstable and subject to environmental deterioration. The National Wastelands Development Board (1985) suggests that "any land which is not producing green biomass consistent with the status of soil and water must be treated as wasteland".

The wastelands could also be described as those uncultivated lands which are not under good forest covers, town and other man-made structures. This would thus exclude current fallows but would include lands which are fallow for more than one and less then five years. The terms of descriptive classes do not reveal or indicate the present use or potential productivity or the land quality, capability or suitability (I.Khan, 1987).

Depending on the underlying causes, the condition pertaining to physical characteristics of these lands may differ from place to place. Since India is vast country with varied climate and soil it is not possible to make any generalisation as regards the condition of the degraded lands. The present condition of these lands form as degraded forests, village common land, village common grazing grounds, land on roadsides,canal sides and railway line sides, marginal agricultural land, saline alkaline lands, waterlogged lands, ravine lands, abandoned mining areas, sand dunes, alpine pastures. cold desert, etc.

Estimates of Wastelands

No comprehensive survey of land-use has so far been carried out for the entire country and, therefore, it is difficult to rely upon the available statistics. Nevertheless it is a fact that large lands are lying in varying degrees of degradation all over the country. Some attempts were made in the past to survey wastelands and blocks of more than 100 hectares of such lands were located in 12 States comprising 6,41,000 hectares. It was found that more than a half of the area was concentrated in the Punjab, Madhya Pradesh, and Uttar Pradesh. Under another scheme a survey of wastelands occuring in five to 100 hectares blocks, was carried out and it was estimated that the extent of such areas (block) in different States was 2.3 million hectares (NCA 1976).

A number of estimates on the extent of wastelands have been made. According to Gadgil *et al.* (1982) 48 million hectares of forests, 17 million hectares of culturable wastes and 23 million hectares of fallow land, that is, a total of 88 million hectares of land are more or less completely unproductive. According to Vohra (1978) 35 million hectares of forests, four million hectares of miscellaneous tree crops, 13 million hectares of permanent pastures, 17 million hectares of culturable wastes and 26 million hectares of fallows that is, a total of 95 million hectares of land represent more or less denuded land surfaces.

According to the National Wastelands Development Board, 175 million hectares are wastelands which include 40 to 60 million hectares of agricultural land, 40 million hectares of degraded forests. Bhumla and Khare have estimated 87.7 million hectares of wastelands (non-forest) which included barren (uncultivated) 7.15 million hectares, cultivable waste 16.22 million hectares, pasture and grazing lands 11.98 million hectares, current fallows 6.02 million hectares, fallows other than current fallows 8.48 million hectares and net area sown 37.87 million hectares.

A criterion which has been used to classify or define wastelands is qualitative. The land affected due to salinity and both water and wind erosion are included in the wastelands. About 94 million hectares have been estimated to be wasted land for these reasons (Bhumbla & Khare). If 36 million hectares of degraded forests are added to these, a total of 130 million hectares would be the estimate for wastelands.

Benthey (1984) has estimated that 200 million hectares are partially degraded in terms of short-term productivity. Of these degraded lands, as many as 100 million hectares produce 20 per cent or less of the dry weight biological potential. Rajasthan and Madhya Pradesh have approximately 20 million hectares of wastelands in each State, which are followed by Maharashtra 14 million hectares. Andhra Pradesh 11 million hectares, Karnataka 9.2 million hectares, Uttar Pradesh 8.1 million and Gujarat 7.8 million hectares. These data are also based on certain assumptions and official statistics. Their actual location on ground has to be ascertained and identified at field level.

In the absence of reliable data-base any conclusion on the availability of wastelands for bringing under vegetative cover would not be more than a crude guess. Whenever the field surveys have been carried out, large discrepancies were detected in the official records, when compared with the results of the survey, in so far as the non-forest wastelands were covered. Large area of wastelands are under encroachments and have been brought under plough. Such lands are still being shown as public lands in Government records. The wastelands which may ultimately be available for development would not be more than 80 million hectares, bulk of which are degraded forests and marginal agricultural lands. The lands most easily available would be degraded forests (Irshad Khan, 1987).

A nation-wide aerial mapping of wastelands has recently been carried out. Figures based on this survey indicate that the total extent of wastelands is only 55 million hectares. However, the Institute for Coastal and Offshore Research which prepared the estimate points out that it is likely to err on the lower side because of the small scale of the maps used by the National Remote Sensing Agency (Table 3.1).

TABLE 3.1: Aerial estimation of wastelands (Nation-wide)

Sl. No.	Description	Million ha
1.	Salt-affected land	3.99
2.	Gullied or ravinous land	6.73
3.	Undulating upland with or without scrub	11.74
4.	Jhum or Forest Blank	6.24
5.	Sandy Area	13.94
6.	Barren Hill-Ridge or Rock outcrop	2.70
7.	Snow covered or Glacial Area	10.07
8.	Total	55.41
	Percentage of State Area	16.852%

Source: Institute for Coastal and Offshore Research.

According to the State-wise break up, the State with the greatest percentage of its area that is classified as wasteland is Rajasthan with 45 per cent, followed by the hill States Jammu and Kashmir, Tripura, Himachal Pradesh, Manipur, Sikkim, Mizoram, Meghalaya and Nagaland. This predominance of the hill States at the top of the list is because of the extent of snow-covered and glacial land in these States (Table 3.2).

TABLE 3.2: Aerial estimation of wastelands, Statewise

Sl. No.	State	Description	Million ha
1	2	3	4
1.	RAJASTHAN	Salt affected land	497.640
		Gullied or Ravinous Land	8766.120
		Undulating Upland with or without scrub	7656
		Sandy Area	130193.938
		Barren Hill Ridge of Rock outcrop	7770.840
		TOTAL	154884.538
		Percentage of State area	45.258
2.	JAMMU & KASHMIR	Salt affected Land	38.280
		Undulating Upland with or without scrub	76.560
		Jhum or Forest Blank	2373.360
		Barren Hill Ridge or Rock outcrop	153.120
		Snow covered or Glacial Area	70054.141
		TOTAL	72695.461
		Percentage of State Area	32.710

(*Contd.*)

TABLE 3.2 (*Contd.*)

1	2	3	4
3.	TRIPURA	Undulating Upland with or without scrub	382.800
		Jhum or Forest Blank	2641.320
		Snow covered or Glacial Area	229.680
		TOTAL	3253.800
		Percentage of State Area	31.056
4.	HIMACHAL PRADESH	Undulating Upland with or without scrub	459.360
		Jhum or Forest Blank	99.280
		Snow covered Glacial Area	13589.800
		TOTAL	15044.440
		Percentage of State Area	27.022
5.	MANIPUR	Undulating Upland with or without scrub	306.240
		Jhum or Forest Blank	5014.680
		Barren Hill Ridge or Rock outcrop	344.520
		TOTAL	5665.440)
		Percentage of State Area	25.340
6.	SIKKIM	Undulating Upland with or without scrub	765.600
		Snow covered or Glacial Area	1077.840
		TOTAL	1843.440
		Percentage of State Area	25.256
7.	MIZORAM	Jhum or Forest Blank	3981.120
		Show covered or Glacial Area	497.640
		TOTAL	4478.760
		Percentage of State Area	21.238
8.	MEGHALAYA	Jhum or Forest Blank	4555.320
		Barren Hill Ridge or Rock outcrop	191.400
		TOTAL	4746.720
		Percentage of State Area	21.106

(*Contd.*)

TABLE 3.2 (*Contd.*)

1	2	3	4
9.	NAGALAND	Jhum or Forest Blank	3253.800
		TOTAL	3253.800
		Percentage of State Area	19.686
10.	GUJARAT	Salt affected land	1110.120
		Gullied or Ravinous Land	191.400
		Jhum or Forest Blank	76.560
		Sandy Area	1492.920
		Barren Hill Ridge or Rock outcrop	842.160
		TOTAL	3713.160
		Percentage of State Area	18.396
11.	ARUNACHAL PRADESH	Undulating Upland with or without scrub	191.400
		Jhum or Forest Blank	5512.320
		Snow covered or Glacial Area	7732.560
		TOTAL	13436.280
		Percentage of State Area	16.076
12.	UTTAR PRADESH	Salt affected Land	19407.961
		Gullied or Ravinous land	8842.680
		Undulating Upland with or without scrub	880.440
		Sandy Area	918.720
		Barren Hill Ridge or Rock Outcrop	880.440
		Snow covered or Glacial Area	7043.520
		TOTAL	40768.201
		Percentage of State Area	13.846
13.	KERALA	Undulating Upland with or without scrub	803.880
		Jhum or Forest Blank	3484.480
		Barren hill Ridge or Rock outcrop	918.720
		Snow covered or Glacial area	114.840
		TOTAL	5320.920
		Percentage of State Area	13.690

(*Contd.*)

TABLE 3.2 (*Contd.*)

1	2	3	4
14.	TAMIL NADU	Salt affected Land	574.200
		Gullied or Ravinous land	4210.800
		Undulating Upland with or without scrub	6507.600
		Sandy Area	1914
		Barren Hill Ridge or Rock outcrop	1071.840
		TOTAL	17610.800
		Percentage of State Area	13.538
15.	ORISSA	Salt affected land	153.120
		Undulating Upland with or without scrub	12326.160
		Jhum or Forest Blank	6622.440
		Sandy Area	382.800
		TOTAL	19484.520
		Percentage of State Area	12.506
16.	KARNATAKA	Salt affected land	267.960
		Gullied or Ravinous Land	2220.240
		Undulating Upland with or without scrub	12517.560
		Jhum or Forest Blank	3100.680
		Barren hill Ridge or Rock outcrop	3828
		TOTAL	21934.440
		Percentage of State Area	11.436
17.	ANDHRA PRADESH	Salt affected Land	880.440
		Gullied or Ravinous Land	4517.040
		Undulating Upland with or without scrub	18642.359
		Jhum or Forest Blank	880.440
		Sandy Area	1033.560
		Barren Hill Ridge or Rock outcrop	4708.440
		TOTAL	30662.279
		Percentage of State Area	11.076

(*Contd.*)

TABLE 3.2 (*Contd.*)

1	2	3	4
18.	MADHYA PRADESH	Gullied or Ravinous Land	21283.680
		Undulating Upland with or without scrub	13436.280
		Jhum or Forest Blank	7005.240
		Barren Hill Ridge or Rock outcrop	2411.840
		TOTAL	44137.040
		Percentage of State Area	9.966
19.	MAHARASHTRA	Salt affected Land	1186.680
		Gullied or Ravinous Land	7388.040
		Undulating Upland with or without scrub	19637.641
		Jhum or Forest Blank	1454.640
		Barren Hill Ridge or Rock outcrop	995.280
		TOTAL	30662.281
		Percentage of State Area	9.962
20.	GOA, DAMAN AND DIU	Undulating Upland with or without scrub	306.240
		Jhum or Forest Blank	38.280
		TOTAL	344.520
		Percentage of State Area	9.034
21.	HARYANA	Salt affected Land	1110.120
		Gullied or Ravinous Land	191.400
		Jhum or Forest Blank	76.560
		Sandy Area	1492.920
		Barren Hill Ridge or Rock outcrop	842.160
		TOTAL	3713.160
		Percentage of State Area	8.396
22.	BIHAR	Gullied or Ravinous Land	1875.720
		Undulating Upland with or without scrub	8727.840
		Jhum or Forest Blank	2373.360
		Barren Hill Ridge or Rock outcrop	2335.080
		TOTAL	15312.000
		Percentage of State Area	8.806

(*Contd.*)

TABLE 3.2 (*Contd.*)

1	2	3	4
23.	PUNJAB (including Chandigarh)	Salt affected Land	1301.520
		Sandy Area	2603.040
		TOTAL	19484.560
		Percentage of State Area	7.730
24.	WEST BENGAL	Salt affected land	1263.240
		Undulating Upland with or without scrub	4249.080
		Jhum or Forest Blank	535.920
		Barren Hill Ridge or Rock outcrop	306.240
		TOTAL	6354.480
		Percentage of State Area	7.232
25.	ASSAM	Undulating Upland with of of without scrub	574.200
		Jhum or Forest Blank	2373.360
		TOTAL	2947.560
		Percentage of State Area	3.752

* *Source:* Centre for Science and Environment (1986).

Distribution of Wastelands into Agro-climatic Regions

As stated earlier the actual geographical location of wastelands have to be ascertained and identified at the field level. Any gross assumption will lead to a miscalculation since there are no fixed boundaries from where a particular wasteland starts or ends. India has been divided into 127 agro-climatic zones. The objectives for demarcation these zones have been varied and based on certain agro-climatical considerations. To consider these zones as a base for the distribution and location of wastelands will not fulfil any purpose either for planning or development of these lands. Wastelands are spread over to the wider areas not only beyond the limits of these zones but the States where they are located. The zonal statistics for the availability of wastelands is not available. However, the major concentration of the wastelands in and around these zones can be identified. The information on wastelands as imputed for the National Remote Sensing Agency's survey can further be used into different agro-climatic zones developed by the ICAR project on National Agricultural Research Project. The zones having different wastelands are shown in Table 3.3.

TABLE 3.3: Distribution of wastelands into agro-climatic zones

State	Agro-climatic zones having large area of wastelands	Major forms of wastelands
1	2	3
I. Andhra Pradesh	1. Scare Rainfall zone Rayalaseema 2. Southern Telengana zone 3. North Telengana zone	1. Ravines 2. Undulating Uplands 3. Salt affected 4. Jhum cultivation
II. Bihar	1. Central and North Eastern Plateau Zone 2. Western Plateau Zone 3. South Eastern Plateau Zibe	1. Ravines 2. Undulating Uplands 3. Jhum cultivation
III. Gujarat	1. North Gujarat Zone 2. North West Zone 3. North Southern Zone 4. South Saurashtra Zone 5. Middle Gujarat Zone	1. Salt affected 2. Ravines 3. Sandy
IV. Haryana	1. Western Zone 2. Eastern Zone	1. Salt affected 2. Sandy 3. Ravines
V. Jammu & Kashmir	1. Cold Arid Zone	1. Sandy 2. Jhum cultivation
VI. Karnataka	1. North Eastern Transition Zone 2. North East Dry zone 3. Northern Dry Zone 4. Central Dry Zone 5. Eastern Dry Zone 6. Southern Dry Zone	1. Ravines 2. Undulating 3. Jhum cultivation
VII. Kerala	1. Central Zone	1. Jhum cultivation
VIII. Madhya Pradesh	1. Bundelkhand Zone 2. Chattisgarh Plain Zone 3. Gird Zone 4. North Hill Zone Chattisgarh	1. Ravines 2. Undulating Uplands 3. Jhum cultivation
IX. Maharashtra	1. Scarcity Zone 2. Central Maharashtra Plateau Zone 3. Contral Vidharbha Zone	1. Ravines 2. Undulating Uplands 3. Jhum cultivation

(Contd.)

TABLE 3.3 (*Contd.*)

1	2	3
X. Orissa	1. Western Undulating Zone 2. West Central Table land Zone 3. North Eastern Plateau Zone 4. North Central Plateau Zone	1. Undulating Uplands 2. Jhum Cultivation
XI. Punjab	1. Western Zone 2. Central Plain Zone 3. Western Plain Zone	1. Salt affected 2. Sandy
XII. Rajasthan	1. Arid Western Plain Zone 2. Transitional Plain Zone of Inland Zone 3. Transitional Plain Zone of Luni basin 4. Semi Arid Eastern Zone 5. Flood Prone Eastern Plain Zone	1. Salt affected 2. Ravines 3. Sandy 4. Undulating Uplands
XIII. Tamil Nadu	1. North Eastern Zone 2. North Western Zone 3. Western Zone	1. Ravines 2. Sandy 3. Jhum Cultivation
XIV. Uttar Pradesh	1. South Western Semi Arid Zone 2. Bundelkhand Zone 3. Central Plain Zone 4. Vindhyan Zone	1. Salt affected 2. Ravines 3. Sandy
XV. West Bengal	1. Coastal Saline Zone 2. Laterite and Red soil Zone	1. Salt affected 2. Undulating Uplands

The above zones have only those classes of wastelands where possibilities of energy plantations can be foreseen. The hilly States of Himachal Pradesh, Sikkim, Meghalaya, Mizoram, Tripura, Nagaland and Arunachal Pradesh where large areas under wasteland classification fall either under the barren hill ridges or snow covered (glacial area) have not been included in the list. The afforestation under these terrain conditions is not possible. Sandy dunes of Rajasthan and soils of extremely dry and cold climate of Ladakh region of Jammu & Kashmir States are also part of the country where planting fuelwood species have not prospects at the present.

High Propensity Wasteland Districts

The National Wasteland Development Board in collaboraton with the

Department of Space, Survey of India and Ministry of Defence have identified the high propensity wastelands districts in the country. The detailed maps of these 146 districts having more than 15 per cent of their total geographical area under wastelands have been prepared. In the first round for five of the districts (Dungarpur, Sundargarh, Purulia, Bellary and Almora), with the help of maps and available information, the detailed action plans are underway for the reclaiming process. The NWDB expects to develop a perfect methodology for the preparation of detailed plans. On the basis of this experiment remaining 141 districts will be taken in the second round of action plan (Table 3.4).

TABLE 3.4: High propensity wastelands districts in the country

Sl. No.	State	Districts
1	2	3
1.	Andhra Pradesh	Nizamabad, Vizianagram, Karimnagar, Chittor, Rangareddy, Medak, Cuddapah, Vishakhapatnam, Mahaboobnagar, Prakasam, Nalgonda, Kurnool, Ananthapur and Nellore
2.	Assam	Haflong (North Cachar) and Diphu (Karbi Anglong)
3.	Bihar	Singhbum, Dhanbad, Nawada, Siwan, Vaishally, Muzaffarpur, Sasaram, Palamau and Aurangabad
4.	Gujarat	Jam Nagar, Junagadh, Bhavnagar, Gandhinagar, Kheda, Ahmedabad, Mehsana, Panchmahal, Surendra Nagar and Rajkot
5.	Haryana	Sirsa, Karnal, Hissar, Jind and Gurgaon
6.	Himachal Pradesh	Hamirpur, Dharamsala and Chamba
7.	Jammu & Kashmir	Udhampur
8.	Karnataka	Kolar, Belgaum, Raichur, Bellary, Chitradurga, Hassan, Tumkur and Bangalore
9.	Kerala	Kasargod, Cannanore, Palghat, Wyanad, Idukki and Malapuram
10.	Maharashtra	Dhule, Kolhapur, Jalgaon, Ahmednagar, Ratnagiri, Satara, Pune, Sangli, Thana and Nasik

(*Contd.*)

TABLE 3.4 (*Contd.*)

1	2	3
11.	Madhya Pradesh	Bhind, Raisen, Narasingpur, Indore, Shajapur, Ujjain, Mandsaur, Rajgarh, Rajnandgaon, Ratlam, Raipur, Durg, Guna, Datia, Vidisha, Dewas, Rewa and Tikamgarh
12.	Manipur	Karong and Imphal
13.	Nagaland	Kohima, Mokokchung and Zunhebote
14.	Orissa	Ganjam, Cuttack, Bhubaneshwar, Dhenkanal, Sundargarh, Bolangir and Kalahandi
15.	Punjab	Sangrur, Kapurthala and Bhatinda
16.	Rajasthan	Pali, Tonk, Jodhpur, Churu, Ajmer, Sawai Madhopur, Bundi, Jhalawar, Kota, Udaipur, Dungarpur and Bhilwara
17.	Tamil Nadu	North Arkot, Periyar, Tiruchirapilli, Madurai, Dharampuri, Salem and Ramana Thapuram
18.	Uttar Pradesh	Fatehpur, Kanpur, Etah, Agra, Aligarh, Varanasi, Lucknow, Ghazipur, Azamgarh, Allahabad, Ballia, Pratapgarh, Hamirpur, Unnao, Mainpuri, Ettawa, Jhansi, Lalitpur, Rae Barelli, Farukhabad, Sultanpur, Jaunpur, Jalaun and Bulandshahr
19.	West Bengal	Midnapore, Purulia and Bankura

Institutional Arrangements for Wasteland Development

The National Land Use and Wasteland Development Council held its first meeting in February 1986. After this meeting the State/UT governments were advised to constitute Nodal Agencies for wasteland development programme. It was advised that at the highest level, a body on the lines of Council or the NWDB which could be chaired by the Chief Minister or subject-matter minister. At the next level a Coordination Committee or Steering Committee which could be chaired by the Chief Secretary/Agriculture Production Commissioner or any other appropriate senior government official.

Many States/UTs have taken action on NWDB's recommendations and had set up Boards/Committees, others have assigned the responsibility of wasteland development to the existing bodies within their set up, like State Land Use Board, Town and Country Planning Board, State Planning Commission etc. (See Annexure 3.10). These bodies meet to constantly review and direct various departmental programmes so that they can effectively integrate in support of the wasteland development and afforestation efforts.

ANNEXURE 3.1

Estimates of Wastelands in India

(Hectares in million)

States/UTs	Non-forest degraded area	Forest degraded area*	Total
(1)	(2)	(3)	(4)
Andhra Pradesh	7.682	3.734	11.416
Assam	0.935	0.795	1.730
Bihar	3.896	1.562	5.458
Gujarat	7.153	0.683	7.836
Haryana	2.401	0.074	2.475
Himachal Pradesh	1.424	0.534	1.958
Jammu & Kashmir	0.531	1.034	1.565
Karnataka	7.122	2.043	9.165
Kerala	1.053	0.226	1.279
Madhya Pradesh	12.947	7.195	20.142
Maharashtra	11.560	2.841	14.401
Manipur	0.014	1.424	1.438
Meghalaya	0.815	1.103	1.918
Nagaland	0.508	0.878	1.386
Orissa	3.157	3.227	6.384
Punjab	1.151	0.079	1.230
Rajasthan	18.010	1.933	19.943
Sikkim	0.131	0.150	0.281
Tamil Nadu	3.392	1.009	4.401
Tripura	0.108	0.865	0.973
Uttar Pradesh	6.635	1.426	8.061
West Bengal	2.177	0.359	2.536
UTs	0.889	2.715	3.604
Total	93.691	35.889	129.580

* Barren area notified as forests not included in the above figures.

Source: D.R. Bhumbla and A. Khare.

ANNEXURE 3.2

Estimates of Wastelands in India (Non-forest area only)

(Hectares in thousand)

States/UTs	Saline & alkaline lands	Wind eroded area	Water eroded area	Total
Andhra Pradesh	240	—	7442	7682
Assam	—	—	935	935
Bihar	004	—	3892	3896
Gujarat	1214	704	5235	7153
Haryana	526	1599	276	2401
Himachal Pradesh	—	—	1424	1424
Jammu & Kashmir	—	—	531	531
Karnataka	404	—	6718	7122
Kerala	016	—	1037	1053
Madhya Pradesh	242	—	12705	12947
Maharashtra	534	—	11026	11560
Manipur	—	—	014	014
Meghalaya	—	—	815	815
Nagaland	—	—	508	508
Orissa	404	—	2753	3157
Punjab	688	—	463	1151
Rajasthan	728	10623	6659	18010
Sikkim	—	—	131	131
Tamil Nadu	004	—	3388	3392
Tripura	—	—	108	108
Uttar Pradesh	1295	—	5340	6635
West Bengal	850	—	1327	2177
UTs	16	—	873	889
Total	7165	12926	73600	93691

Source: D.R. Bhumbla and A. Khare.

ANNEXURE 3.3

Wind Eroded Regions in India (Non-Forest Only)

(lac ha)

State Districts	Net Area sown	P & G	CW	Fallows	Current Fallows
I. *Rajasthan*					
1. Bikaner	2.91	0.42	14.27	1.65	1.24
2. Jaisalmer	7.45	0.89	34.84	0.77	0.66
3. Barmer	1.51	2.12	37.75	2.87	2.21
4. Jodhpur	4.26	1.12	0.09	4.97	2.30
5. Nagaur	5.51	0.73	0.03	0.96	2.84
6. Churu	3.38	0.47	0.44	1.28	1.37
7. Pali	1.15	0.92	0.16	1.31	1.40
8. Jalore	2.45	0.51	0.06	1.07	1.08
9. Ganganagar	1.21	0.22	2.50	0.35	0.62
10. Jhunjhunu	3.00	0.45	0.05	0.17	0.32
11. Sikar	4.88	0.48	0.14	0.46	0.74
Total	37.71	8.33	56.33	15.63	14.18
II. *Gujarat*					
1. Mehsana	6.96	0.56	0.27	0.12	0.26
2. Banaskantha	8.21	0.72	0.37	0.11	0.60
3. Kutch	3.00	0.70	1.80	1.60	0.45
Total	18.17	1.98	2.44	1.83	1.31
III. *Haryana*					
1. Bhiwani	4.51	0.08	—	—	0.05
2. Hissar	5.42	—	—	—	5.42
3. Rohtak	3.27	—	0.15	—	0.08
Total	13.20	0.08	0.15	—	0.42
Grand Total	69.08	10.39	58.92	17.46	15.91
Wind eroded area:	Net sown area		(50%)	—	34.54
	P & G (100%)	—	—	10.39	
	C W (100%)	—	—	58.92	
	Fallow (100%)	—	—	17.46	
	Current Fallows	—	—	7.95	
	Total			129.26	

P & G: Pasture and Grazing : CW : Culturable waste.

Source: D.R. Bhumbla and A. Khare.

ANNEXURE 3.4

Statewise Distribution of Arid and Semi-Arid Areas

State	Arid (km^2)	Semi-arid (km^2)	Percentage	
			Arid	Semi arid
Hot				
Rajasthan	1,96,150	1,21,020	61	13
Gujarat	62,180	90,520	19.6	9
Punjab & Haryana	27,350	58,650	9	6
Maharashtra	1,290	1,89,580	0.4	19
Karnataka	8,570	1,39,360	3	15
Andhra Pradesh	21,560	1,38,670	7	15
Tamil Nadu	—	95,250	—	10
Uttar Pradesh	—	64,230	—	7
Madhya Pradesh	—	59,470	—	6
Cold				
Jammu & Kashmir	78,300	13,780	—	—
Total	3,95,390	9,70,530	—	—
Total area of India	32,82,016		12.05	29.57

Source: H.S. Mann and K.D. Muthana (1984).

ANNEXURE 3.5

Geographical Distribution of Salt-Affected Soils in India

Broad Groups	States	Approx. Area (million ha)
1. Coastal salt-affected soils		
(a) Coastal salt-affected soil of arid region	Gujarat	0.714
(b) Deltaic coastal salt affected soils of the humid region	West Bengal, Orissa, Andhra Pradesh and Tamil Nadu	1,394
(c) Acid salt-affected soils	Kerala	0.016
2. Salt-affected soils of the medium and deep black soil regions	Karnataka, MP, Andhra Pradesh and Maharashtra	1,420
3. Salt-affected soils of the arid and semi-arid regions	Gujarat, Rajasthan, Punjab Haryana and UP	1,000
4. Sodic Soils of the Indo-gangetic plains	Haryana, Punjab, UP, Bihar, Rajasthan and MP	2,500
Total		7,044

Source: I.P. Abrol and H.S. Gill (1983).

ANNEXURE 3.6

Extent of Coastal Saline Soils in India

States (Districts)	Area (million hectare)
West Bengal (24 Parganas North, 24 Parganas South, Midnapur East, Howrah)	0.820
Gujarat (Surat, Valsad, Bharuch, Kaira, Ahmedabad, Bhavnagar, Surendranagar, Amreli, Rajkot, Jamnagar and Junagadh)	0.714
Kutch region	—
Orissa (Balasore, Cuttack, Puri, Ganjam)	0.400
Andhra Pradesh (Srikakulam, Vizianagram, Vishakhapatnam, East Godavari, West Godavari, Krishna, Guntur, Prakasam and Nellore)	0.276
Tamil Nadu (Chengelput, South Arcot, Tanjavore, Ramnathapuram, Tirunelvely)	0.100
Karnataka (North & South Canara)	0.086
Maharashtra (Ratnagiri, Sindhudurg, Raigad, Thane)	0.064
Kerala (Ernakulam, Alleppey, Cannanore and other coastal districts)	0.026
Goa	0.018
A & N Islands	0.015
Pondicherry	0.001
Mangrove	0.574
	3.094

Source: Yadav et al. (1983) & Bandopadhyay and Abrol, (1984).

ANNEXURE 3.7

Districtwise Area of Ravines in Uttar Pradesh

District	Ravine area (hectares)
Agra	1,78,000
Aligarh	14,000
Allahabad	16,000
Banda	1,20,000
Barabanki	9,000
Bulandshahr	5,000
Etawah	1,58,000
Farrukhabad	40,000
Fatehpur	31,000
Mirzapur	76,000
Muzaffarnagar	19,000
Hamirpur	1,29,000
Jalaun	1,14,000
Jaunpur	13,000
Jhansi	1,29,000
Kanpur	14,000
Lucknow	13,000
Mainpuri	39,000
Mathura	14,000
Meerut	6,000
Rai Bareli	9,000
Varanasi	18,000
Total area	12,30,000

Source: A.N. Chaturvedi (1985).

ANNEXURE 3.8

Area of Ravines by Catchment of Rivers in U.P.

River	Ravine area (hectares)
Yamuna	3,89,000
Chambal	79,000
Kali	89,000
Ken	20,000
Gomti	32,000
Sengar	51,000
Betwa	2,27,000
Dhasan	51,000
Pahuj	53,000
Sal	29,000
Ganga	35,000
Son	77,000
Kaveri	50,000
Sindh	48,000

Source: A.N. Chaturvedi (1985).

ANNEXURE 3.9

Area Under Ravines in the States

State	Area in (lakh hectares)
Uttar Pradesh	12.30
Madhya Pradesh	6.83
Bihar	6.00
Rajasthan	4.52
Gujarat	4.00
Punjab	1.20
West Bengal	1.01
Tamil Nadu	0.60

Source: H.S. Sharma (1980).

ANNEXURE 3.10

Institutional Arrangements in States/Union Territories for Wastelands Development

Sl. No.	State/UT	Council/Board	Coordination Committee
1	2	3	4
1.	Andhra Pradesh	State Land Use Board in existence	—
2.	Assam	State Land Use and Wastelands Development Council, Chairman: Chief Minister	State Wastelands Development Board, Chairman: Commissioner, Planning & Development Dept.
3.	Bihar	Wastelands Development Board	—
4.	Gujarat	Land Use Board	High Powered Committee on Wastelands, Chairman: Chief Secretary
5.	Haryana	State Land Use Board	—
6.	Himachal Pradesh	Land Use Board	—
7.	Jammu & Kashmir	—	Coordination Committee for Wastelands Development, Chairman: Chief Secretary
8.	Karnataka	State Land Use Board	High Powered Committee on Wastelands, Chairman: Chief Secretary
9.	Kerala	State Land Use & Development Council	State Level Coordination Committee Chairman: Agri. Prod. Commissioner
10.	Madhya Pradesh	State Land Use & Wastelands Development Council	—
11.	Maharashtra	State Land Use Board	Committee on Wastelands, Chairman: Minister Incharge of Social Forestry.

(Contd.)

ANNEXURE 3.10 (*Contd.*)

1	2	3	4
12.	Manipur	State Land Use Board	—
13.	Meghalaya	State Land Use Board	—
14.	Nagaland	No separate organisation	Committee considered not necessary.
15.	Orissa	State Land Use & Wastelands Development Council	State Coordination Committee for Wastelands Development Plantation & Orchard Programmes, Chairman: Commissioner Agrl. & Rural Development.
16.	Punjab	State Land Use Board and Wastelands Development Board	Implementation Committee, Chairman: Financial Commissioner.
17.	Rajasthan	—	Committee of Direction for Wastelands Development, Chairman: Chief Secretary
18.	Sikkim	State Land Use and Environment Board	—
19.	Tamil Nadu	State Planning Commission Board	Afforestation and Wastelands Dev. Committee, Chairman: Chief Secretary
20.	Tripura	State Land Use Board	—
21.	Uttar Pradesh	State Land Use Board	State Level Committee, Chairman: Agri. Prod. Commissioner.
22.	West Bengal	—	Committee of Direction, Chairman: Member of Revenue
23.	A & N Islands	—	—
24.	Arunachal Pradesh	Wastelands Development Council	—

(*Contd.*)

ANNEXURE 3.10 (*Contd.*)

1	2	3	4
25.	Chandigarh	Has very small area under forests; hence, not consulted	—
26.	Dadra & Nagar Haveli	Extent of wastelands is almost negligible. As such need not felt.	—
27.	Delhi	Land Use Board	Coordination Committee, Chairman: Chief Secretary
28.	Goa, Daman & Diu	Town & Country Planning Board	High Powered Committee of Direction, Chairman: Chief Secretary
29.	Mizoram	State Land Use Board	—
30.	Lakshadweep	Entire area under thick cultivation. Therefore, there is no scope for setting up a Council	—
31.	Pondicherry	Land Use Board	Coordination and Monitoring Committee, Chairman: Development Commissioner.

Source: NWDB.

ANNEXURE 3.11

Characteristics of the Major Wasteland Areas

The Desert Areas

The arid zone of India occupies an area of about 31.7 m hectares of hot desert in Rajasthan, Gujarat and Haryana; besides 10m hectares of cold desert in Ladakh, Lahaul and Spiti in the north. Out of the former, an area of about 18m hectares is the core of the desert especially in Bikaner, Jaisalmer, Barmer, Jodhpur, Nagaur, Churu, Pali and Jalore districts. The Rajasthan desert fulfils in a large measure, though not in a rigorous sense, the general characteristics of a desert, viz. low rainfall with a large variability, large diurnal temperature variation, high evaporation, non-existence of a perennial river, scanty vegetation, very little agriculture, dependence of man on animals and sparse and nomadic population.

Average annual rainfall of the region varies from 150 to 500 mm decreasing from east to west, with a coefficient of variation of 60 to 70 per cent. Most of the rainfall occurs erratically, from July to September. The mean daily maximum temperature in the summer is generally 40°C and during the winter varies from 22 to 28°C. The mean daily minimum temperature varies from 24 to 26°C during summer and 4 to 10°C during winter.

The mean diurnal temperature variation ranges from 12 to 17°C The mean relative humidity during the summer varies from 36 to 50 per cent, and from 66 to 78 per cent during the monsoon in the morning hours. In the afternoon, however, there is a drop and the mean values range from 20 to 35 per cent during summer and 48 to 60 per cent in the monsoon season. The mean evaporation during summer exceeds 10 mm per day. The potential evapotranspiration values during summer vary from 7 to 9 mm per day. The mean daily wind speed is recorded to be highest during summer and monsoon seasons being 8 to 20 km/hr.

The first rational approach to an understanding of the great Indian desert and its problems originated from the First Five Year Plan. According to this, topographical surveys showed the spreading of the desert at the rate of 800 metres per year for the previous 50 years and its encroachment upon approximately 13,000 hectare of fertile land every year. Following this note of alarm, the National Institute of Science arranged in 1952 a comprehensive seminar on Rajasthan desert in which this particular situation was specially discussed from all possible angles. The principal finding of these deliberations was that the desert, as it presents itself now, is the result of meteorological, geological and hydrological changes over the centuries, for which evidences are not lacking, but the desertic condition has undoubtedly been accentuated by the activities of man. As pointed out by Mann, the notion that the Rajasthan desert has been advancing is fairly widespread, but lacks scientific unanimity, mostly because of terminological controversies. The increase and decrease in windblown surfaces have been illustrated by a comparison of old and recent surveys maps which indicated an extension of the desert towards the east. However, the fact that in some areas sand formations have developed, whereas in others they have finished or vanished is no conclusive proof of the movement of the desert. Scientists are unanimous, however, with regard to the accentuation of exric conditions within the desert owing to over exploitation of the vegetation and land resources.

The major factors of desertification are the escalation of human and livestock population and their activities, besides the climatic and geomorphological factors. The human population within the Rajasthan desert has increased a growth rate of 158 per cent, the corresponding rate in comparison for the whole of the Rajasthan State being 125 per cent.

The increasing human population is a serious stress, particularly on the vegetal resources of the desert. The seeds of grasses, e.g. *panicum turgidum, P. antidotale, Cenchrus biflorus and Echinochloa colonum,* are mixed with millet for making chapatis (unleavened cakes) especially during drought years, as these are supposed to add to the nutritive value of the food. The intensity with which seed collection is made for direct human consumption throughout the desert region seriously affects the natural process of regeneration of the desirable plant species in the inhospitable terrain.

Livestock population far exceeds human population in arid western Rajasthan. Owing to continued droughts with the consequent migration and mortality, the number of cattle fell heavily, but the number of hardy animals, e.g. the goat, increased substantially. This thus not only reveals a preponderance of the goat and sheep population in the arid

Rajasthan, but also point to their increase during the years of drought. The goats are the desert-makers par excellence, eating every bit of green or dry vegetation.

It is estimated that 60 per cent of the area is covered with blown sands, forming sand dune chains, and interdune sand sheet plains. Some of these dunes are stabilised and support some vegetative cover, some are bare with loose sands. Shifting dunes are common, advancing with prevailing south-west winds, and engulfing adjoining cultivated lands, roads and habitations.

Damage from wind erosion is of numerous types. The dust storms resulting there from are, to say the least, disagreeable and often almost unbearable. Fences, ditches and channels are blocked or burried and farmsteads are rendered uninhabitable. Crop damage particularly in the and channels are blocked or burried and farmsteads are rendered uninhabitable. Crop damage particularly in the seedling stage, by blowing soil is often a major concern. Tender seedlings may be completely killed. Often, sufficient soil is removed to expose plant roots or ungerminated seed, and this results in crop failure. Covering of established crops by drifting soils is another common result. There are but a few of the more evident results of wind erosion. The most serious and significant by far, however, is the change in soil texture caused by wind erosion. Finer soil fractions (silt, clay and organic matter) are removed and carried away by the wind leaving the coarser fractions behind. This sorting action not only removes the most important material from the standpoint of productivity and water retention but leaves a more sandy and thus a more erodible soil than the original. Successive removals eventually create a soil condition wherein plant growth is minimised and erodibility greatly increased. Control becomes more and more difficult. In the extreme, the sand begins to drift and form unstable dunes which encroach on better surrounding lands. It is this degradation of soil resources that constitutes the most serious aspect of wind erosion. Uncontrolled, they become a menace to adjacent productive lands.

Ravines

Grim and spectacular evidence of soil erosion is afforded by the ravines of the Yamuna, Chambal, the Mahi, the Sabarmati rivers and their tributaries, where villages once surrounded by fertile fields now lie in a network of ravines, considerable agricultural areas have been laid waste and on the verge of enormous ravines – the peasant fights an apparently losing battle against the forces of nature. There is no historical record to show when the deterioration started but it is reasonable to assume that indiscriminate use of land leading to disturbance of the ecology and environment has been of the reasons for this degradation. Erratic, short duration and high intensity rainfall, loose and friable nature of the soil, steep slopes and undulating terrain, faulty agricultural practices, cutting of trees and bushes, grazing of lands and similar biotic interference have combined to aggravate the situation, ultimately resulting in deep gullies, commonly known as ravines. High flood level has contributed to the deepening and widening of the ravines. The rivers in high floods back up into the ravines and hasten soil slipping. Prolonged inundation causes damage to protective vegetative cover. Ravine formation has damaged fertile cultivable land along the river banks of the region. The process once started continues with increasing speed.

The Planning Commission published a study on survey and reclamation of ravines in India in 1965. In 1972, under the auspices of the Ministry of Home Affairs, Government of India, a working group reported on the ravine problems in the country and advised formulation of a Ravine Reclamation Programme. According to this working group, the area of ravines in four States was as follows:

> Uttar Pradesh — 12.30 lakh ha; Madhya Pradesh — 6.83 lakh ha; Rajasthan — 4.52 lakh ha; and Gujarat — 4.00 lakh ha making a total of 27.65 lakh hectares.

The report of the Working Group gives the districtwise and riverwise distribution of the ravine lands in Uttar Pradesh, Madhya Pradesh and Rajasthan. In Gujarat, the ravine affected lands lie in north, middle and south Gujarat and the districts affected are Baroda, Kaira, Sabarkantha, Mehsana Ahmedabad, Panchmahal, Broach, Surat and Bulsar. The ravine lands in Gujarat have been categorised on the basis of ownership e.g. privately owned ravine lands (60%), Panchayat gauchar land (21%) and Government owned ravine lands (19%).

Along with ravine formation there has been a lowering of the water-table. It has been estimated that as the accumulated result of flooding and scouring, the bed of the Yamuna at Etawah in Uttar Pradesh has been lowered by 80 ft. in the last five centuries with a corresponding fall in the spring level; this is established by the old sugar mills in the Etawah trans-Yamuna area where water level is now far too low to admit of irrigation and also by the fact that in the fort of Shergadh near Auriya, the curb of the large well in use in 1550 is now 60 ft. above mean flood level. The cold weather level of the river is often 120-200 ft below the surrounding country. The uneven and ghastly appearance of the ravines is chiefly due to the peculiar nature of the rock formation, consisting of the clayer soils with intercalated layers of *kankar.* On account of reckless feelings and heavy uncontrolled grazing. The vegetation completely disappeared and serious soil erosion with deep gully and ravine formation started, eating into the cultivated lands. In most of the areas, serious decreases are noticed in the acreages under the agricultural crops wheat, barley and gram and also in the twice cropped areas up to 1945. There is marked and quick deterioration of fertility of the land, destruction of pasturage and a chronic shortage of drinking water in entire ravine areas.

Saline and Alkaline Areas

The factors contributing to the development of these soils are generally arid and semi-arid climate, hard impervious pan in the subsoil region, basin-shaped topography, high water-table, impeded drainage, salt-bearing substrata, excessive canal irrigation, use of saline and brackish water for irrigation and salt-bearing winds in coastal areas. Saline soils or *'Usar'* lands are characterised by occurrence of high proportion of soluble salts usually chlorides and sulphates of the alkali bases. The electrical conductivity of these soils is usually 4m mhos and their pH in the range of 8.0 to 8.5. The soils affected by alkali have a higher pH which may range between 9.0 and 10.5 and the exchangeable sodium may be over 15 per cent. In these cases, the physical condition of the soils is affected considerably due to dispersion of clay colloids which affect their cultivation properties and their cropping capacity. In India, *'Usar'* lands occupy nearly 7 million hectare of area, of which nearly 1.3 million hectare exists in Uttar Pradesh alone.

Water-logged Areas

Water-logging is caused as a result of canal irrigation in areas adjoining agricultural lands where sub-soil water-table steadily rise.

Water-logging conditions are also created in depressions along roadside, canals and railsides during rainy season. Water logging also includes areas which are permanently moist or swampy. Some water-logged areas in low lying depressions contain salt. In India, although exact statistics are not available, water-logged areas occupy an area of about six million ha 3.4 million hectares being subject to surface flooding and 2.6 million hectares with high water-table.

Coastal Region

Soils in this region are sandy, slightly alkaline and poor in nutrients. In some areas, the wind heaps sand into dunes and drives them continually inland on to the fertile crop lands; the rate of accumulation of unprotected sands may be as much as 10 mm in one year as in Digha (West Bengal). Because of the proximity of the sea, the climate is equable and fairly humid (65-80%). In these areas, rainfall varies from 1000 to 5000 mm. This region includes coast of Gujarat, Maharashtra, Karnataka, Goa, West Bengal, Kerala, Orissa, Andhra Pradesh and Tamil Nadu, flanked by the Bay of Bengal on the east and Arabian sea on the west. The Indian Ocean touching the southern tip.

Jhum Cultivation

The sloppy lands in high rainfall areas have traditionally been under the forests. some of these forest lands used to be allocated to crops for 2-3 years after clear felling and burning a patch of forest. This traditional system, called '*Jhum* cultivation' implied that after 2-3 years of cropping, the area under cultivation is abandoned for 15 to 40 years for the regeneration of forest. However, with the increase in population, the period of following to allow regeneration of forests patch by the farmers gets shorter to just 2-3 years; the newly regenerated patch returning to the farmer much earlier and it results in permanent degradation of forest land. The increase in 'jhuming' had led to extensive soil erosion, drought, silting up to rivers and floods in the north-eastern states and areas predominated by tribals in the country.

4

ECONOMICS OF ENERGY PLANTATIONS

From the discussion of the foregoing chapters it is observed that energy plantations have a definite edge on other energy sources in a decentralised rural-based economy where capital investment per work place needs to be low and land utilisation for traditional skills need to be high. Thus, energy plantations have to be designed, managed and operated to provide substantial quantities of fuel continuously throughout the year at costs competitive with other fuels. Hence the necessity of raising and systematically managing energy farms on the wasted lands using right type of species for rapid growth and sustained yield.

To achieve these results, the choice of species is one of the most important factors for the success of energy plantations. The selection of species for a particular area depends on a number of factors like climate, the quantum of annual precipitation and its distribution, type of soil and topography of land. The selected species should have good fuel value and low ash content. These characteristics be combined with the ability to be harvested on short cycle and capacity of reproduction from repeated coppicing. This requires considerable work on energy plantations in respect to identification of species, planting densities, harvesting schedule, influence of cultural factors, treatment etc. Quite a good work has been done in this regard both in western countries (especially in USA and Sweden) as well as in India.

The energy plantation process require a number of field operations till the tree is available for its prime use. These operations are completed with considerable capital expenditure. Broadly, the major activities of operations can be grouped into three heads:

(i) Development and management of fuelwood nurseries;
(ii) Raising plantation at selected sites;
(iii) Production and marketing of fuelwood.

In the following pages these three activities have been studied in detail.

Development and Management of Fuelwood Nurseries

In the first step, the plantation on wastelands for fuelwood requires and establishment of properly sited and well designed nurseries with an irrigation system for production of a sufficient number of seedlings of the required species. These nurseries are of two types: temporary and permanent. The former is established for producing seedlings for two to four years and does not have a permanent infrastructure such as roads buildings and is located near a plantation site. A permanent nursery is established for meeting requirements of seedlings over long periods of time and essentially centralised. For proper management of such a nursery, adequate number of buildings, a well laid out road network and permanent irrigation facilities are developed. A large number of text-books and papers. Irshad Khan (1987), NWDB (1987), Misra (1988), Patel (1988), Hegde (1987) describe nursery practices for forestry plantation in Indian conditions .

The main operations in the establishments of a nursery as recorded and practice include:

- Choosing a nursery site;
- Planning the nursery layout;
- Procurement, storage and pretreatment of seed;
- Soil working in the seed bed or/and container;
- Using fertiliser;
- Sowing seed or/and root cutting;
- Picking out, under-cutting, lifting and transplanting;
- Weeding;
- Protection against pests, diseases, grazing and shading; and
- Packing and despatching seedlings.

Thus many complexities are involved in a nursery work and efficient planning, organisation and control are necessary to meet the demand for seedlings required for plantation.

(i) *Size of Nursery*

About one hectare of nursery is required to produce about 2,00,000 to

2,50,000 plants. The size depends on the number of seedlings required annually, the species, the duration for which a plant remains in a nursery and whether the plants are pricked out in beds or pots.

(ii) *Site Selection*

The most important factors taken into consideration for site selection of a nursery are:

- Soil (texture, drainage);
- Topography and aspect;
- Accessibility;
- Labour and supervisory staff;
- Distance from plantation site.

The good nursery soils are well drained and free working and contain only a little clay or silt. The good soil is sandy or loamy sand. Heavy and clay soils are avoided. A soil having high organic matter content is preferable. It ensures retention of water and nutrients and improves soils workability. The chemical and physical analysis of the soil is done before a nursery is established. The nursery sites are free from weeds and frost hallows and exposed sites are avoided. The sites are preferred on a gentle slope having sufficient gradient which allows rain to run off without causing erosion. Terracing is required in hills where flat ground becomes waterlogged. Sites which are exposed to strong winds are not to be selected unless wind breaks or shelter-belts are ensured to establish. In the hills, the northern and cooler aspects are preferred. The easterly aspect is avoided to protect plants from a possible late spring frost, morning thawing and cold winds. The nursery sites are accessible all the year round by road in order to facilitate transportation of materials required and despatch of plants. Accessibility facilitates brining in of tractors and other machinery. Since nurseries are intensive labour establishment, a labour force is required to establish and maintain a nursery. The number of labourers required depends upon the size, capacity and degree of mechanisation and the general employment situation in the locality.

(iii) *Layout of Nursery*

The shape of the nurseries in most of the cases are square or near square to minimise the length of the boundary and to reduce time in moving from one part to another. The nurseries are divided into a number of sections and their size depending upon the requirement of the seedlings. The permanent nurseries have number of roads and paths. Temporary paths within or between sections are reported about one metre wide. The nursery bed is prepared to grow bare rooted plants or to stack containers or pots. The width of a bed is generally 1 to 1.2 m to facilitate manual tending (hoeing and weeding).

(iv) *Soil Working*

The following operations are carried out in sequence for establishing a new nursery:

- Removal of trees, scrubs and weed growth;
- Ploughing;
- Cleaning;
- Subsoiling;
- Application of fertilizers; and
- Final cultivation.

A new nursery is thoroughly ploughed. Fencing is done after the initial cultivation. The cultivation is preceded by removal of stumps and scrubs if existing on the site. If there are stones, these are removed and clods and lumps are broken. During the cleaning cultivation, levelling is done skilfully on the sloppy sections and if they are flat are made slightly domed. During this operation, however, the large scale moving of the top soil is avoided. In case there are calcareous or iron pan or other layer of soil within 50 cm depth which impede drainage, the dry soils require deep ploughing or subsoiling to restore the drainage system.

Suitable amendments are added in necessary quantities if the soil analysis results show nutrient deficiency or acidity. In case of acidity, lime is applied. If there is phosphorus or magnesium deficiency, mineral phosphate or calcined magnesite are added. Thereafter, the nursery is finally cultivated before seed-beds are prepared. The site then is fenced to protect it against domestic cattle or wild animals.

A good nursery soil has good drainage and is free from stones. The proportion of clay in these nurseries is not more than 10 per cent and that of silt not more than 15 per cent. The texture of soil as such is sandy loam or loamy sand. Soil with high organic matter content forms ideal texture. A good soil structure ensures good drainage and aeration. If the soil structure is lost, the soil becomes compact and dense and losses porosity. Fores in good soil occupy 40-60 per cent volume.

Plant growth is also influenced by soil pH. A pH value 6.5 and 7.5 indicates neutral soil below which it is acidic and above alkaline. Liming makes soil less acidic. But its application is carefully done and any excessive dose prove deleterious.

(v) *Plant Nutrients*

Chemical fertilisers being expensive and, therefore, organic manure is commonly used in nurseries. Excessive application of fertilisers is highly injurious to plant growth. Fertilisers are applied as top dressings or are incorporated into the upper soil by ploughing or retovating. Organic manures such as farmyard manure (FYM) and composts are traditionally used in the country for improving soil fertility.

(vi) *Ground Preparation for Sowing*

After ploughing and levelling seed-beds are laid, the width of seed-beds varied from 1.1 m to 1.2 m and the length generally not exceeding 12 m. Between beds alleys of 50 cm. width are left. They are raised about 10 to 15 cm above ground. However, in the arid and semi-arid areas, the seed-beds are sunken type (10 to 15 cm deep). The longer side of seed-beds is kept in east-west direction. Organic manure or chemical fertiliser in appropriate quantities is applied well in advance. Before sowing, beds are consolidated to enable the soil moisture to reach the surface layers by capillary movement, thereby preventing drying out in warm and dry season. Also any trampling of the beds is avoided.

(vii) *Preparation of Seeds for Sowing*

Good seeds are separated from empty ones by soaking in water for 24 hours. The hellow seeds float on the surface and are removed. However, very minute seeds like that of eucalyptus are difficult to be separate and hence all are sown.

Pre-treatment of seeds is done to break down dormancy and it helps in better seed germination. There are the following methods of pre-treatment and their application differ from species to species:

(1) soaking in water for 24 to 48 hours;
(2) soaking in hot water for 24 hours;
(3) soaking in boiled water for 48 hours;
(4) soaking in sulphuric acid for one hour;
(5) soaking in cold water for two to three days.

(viii) *Seed Sowing*

Seeds are sown in seed-beds, baskets, trays or containers. The sowing times are such that the seedling becomes available for planting in the planting season. A large number of fuelwood species require four to five months for seedling production. In this case, seeds are sown during February - March and the seedlings are ready in July - August. Large seeds are sown by dibbling with a finger or stick to a depth equal to the seed size and the seed is covered by soil (Table 4.1). Very small seeds are very lightly covered like Eucalyptus and are generally sown by broadcast method. After germination, small seedlings are pricked out to other beds or containers. Direct sowing is also done in containers.

(ix) *Raising of Seedlings in Containers*

Containers are of many types. The commonest type is polythene bags (polypots). Others are paper pots, earthen pots, plastic tubes, bamboo pots, baskets etc. The size of polythene bags varies according to preference but they have perforation. The common size are 15 × 20 cm and 20 × 25 cm. Soil is mixed in the right proportion with suitable nutrient application. The filled containers are stacked properly. The container raised seedlings are more labour intensive, but give better survival results.

Arrangements for irrigation are made well in advance. An optimum moisture level is maintained in containers or nursery beds or trays or baskets. The irrigation is done either by flooding or by sprinkling. During dry season, watering is done twice a day. In order to reduce stress caused by evapo-transpiration and high temperature at some places, shading is made available. Growth of weeds affects seedlings and that weeds are controlled by manual weeding.

The seedlings in a nursery are also vulnerable to fungal diseases like damping off and the insect damage. To protect seedlings from such damages, adequate measures are taken. Pesticides such as Aldrin and Dieldin are applied before sowing or are sprayed for controlling defoliators.

Cost of Seedling Raising

The cost of seedling raising at the nurseries for fuelwood species under specific geographical locations have been estimated by a number of researchers Relwani (1981), Chaturvedi (1983), Hedge (1987), NWDB (1987), Misra (1988), Patel (1988) etc. As a practice the small and thinner size of seeds are first sown by the broadcasting method into beds while large and broad seeds by dibbling either direct to the pots or in the beds. The type of sowing in the nurseries differ from species to species according to their seed specifications.

Attempts in Table 4.2 to 4.15 have been made to work out on the different costs involved for the seedling raising. These are based on certain assumptions after having discussions with the researchers and gardeners. Due to large variations in the operational costs, the information thus obtained have been standardized and rounded off and are subject to change for specific locations. The opportunity cost of land and water charges, the two pre-requisites, have not been added to the total cost. It is assumed that the land is freely available along with abandoned supply of water near the nursery site. The labour for irrigation and depreciation on irrigation devices make a part of the total cost. The general information on the species have been obtained from F.R.I. Dehradun (1985). Wages have separately been included accordingly to the operations performed by male and female labourer. The source of quality seed is from Dehradun and Bangalore and seed prices are as prevailed in the market.

In the following pages, operationwise cost for the fourteen most promising fuelwood species have been calculated (Tables 4.2 to 4.15). A 20 bed nursery (10 m × 1.2 m) is developed, for obtaining the number of seedlings to be planted in the wasteland tracts of the country.

In most of the cases, the two major items of expenditure for nursery development together contribute more than 85 per cent of the total cost. This reflects the high predominance of labour use besides the costly item of polybags. In cases where the seeds are thinner and number of seedlings per unit of area raised are more, the cost for polypot's goes high and this increases the higher contribution of polybags to the total expenditure. Almost all the operations are mannual and use of machinery is negligible in the existing conditions; the high labour contribution means more share of labour to the total nursery raising cost.

TABLE 4.1: General information on promising species for fuelwood development

Species	No. of seeds	Sowing season	Seed germination rate (%)	Planting Season
1. *Acacia nilotica/A.tortilis*	6000—8000	March	88	June — July
2. *Albizia lebbeck*	8000—13000	February — July	60—94	July
3. *Azadirachta indica*	3330	July	100	July
4. *Butea monosperma*	9850—14790	May	75—100	July — August
5. *Cassia samea*	37,000	June — August	98	July
6. *Casuarina equisetifolia*	60000—80,000	January — February	70	June
7. *Dalbergia sissoo*	53,000	March	90—100	July — August
8. *Eucalyptus* sps.	90,000—100,000	September — October	90	July
9. *Leucaena leucocephala*	5000—7000	March	50—60	July — August
10. *Pithocellobium dulce*	6700	February — March	45	July — August
11. *Prosopis juliflora*	5000—6000	February — March	60—80	July — August
12. *Tamarindus indica*	1800	April	66	July
13. *Terminalia arjuna*	775	April — May	50—60	June — July
14. *Ziziphus mauritiana*	1240—1760	April — May	31—95	July

Source: F.R.I., Dehradun (1985).

TABLE 4.2: Cost of seedling raising at nurseries — *Eucalyptus* sp.

Species	:	*Eucalyptus* sp.
Method of raising	:	Seed bed and polybag containers
Number of seed beds	:	20 beds
Size of one bed	:	10 m × 1.2 m or 12 sq. metre
Total area of beds	:	240 sq. metres
Assuming distance between seedings	:	7.5 cm × 7.5 cm or .0056 m^2
Space occupied by each plant	:	$\frac{0.0056 \text{ m}^2}{2} = 0.0028 \text{ m}^2$
Number of plants in 240 sq m	:	$\frac{240}{0.0028} = 85.700$
Seed germination rate	:	90 per cent
Mortality rate in beds	:	10 per cent (90% survival rate)
Culling loss	:	15 per cent (85% selected)
Total seeds required for raising 85,700 healthy plants	:	$\frac{85{,}700}{0.90 \times 0.90 \times 0.85} = 1{,}25{,}000$
Number of seeds per kg.	:	90,000 — 100,000 say 95,000
Quantity of seed required	:	1.250 kg
Seed rate	:	Rs. 80 per kg

COST INVOLVED		Rs.	Percentage
* Seed value for 1.250 kg	:	100.00	0.38
* Seed transportation cost	:	25.00	0.09
* Seed treatment	:	25.00	0.09
* Labour required for bed preparation and sowing/broadcasting @ one bed per day per male worker wage rate - Rs. 20 per day	:	400.00	1.53
* Organic manure for beds @ Rs. 45 per cart load — 2 cart loads	:	90.00	0.34
* Coarse sand for beds @ Rs. 10 per cart load — 2 cart loads	:	20.00	0.07
* Irrigation the beds for 30 days by female labour @ Rs. 10 per day	:	300.00	1.15
* Value of poly bags @ 12 paise per bag (85,700 × 0.12)	:	10,284.00	39.31
* Organic manure required for bag filling @ 10000 bags per cart load	:	382.00	1.46
* Coarse sand required for bag filling @ 10,000 bags per cart load	:	85.00	0.32
* Labour required for bag filling including sieving to remove pebbles @ 200 bags per day by female labour	:	4,285.00	16.38
* Pesticides	:	100.00	0.38
* Transplanting of seedlings into poly bags @ 200 plants per day by female labour	:	4,285.00	16.38

(Contd.)

* Irrigating and weeding the poly bags for 60 days by female labour	:	600.00	2.30
* Supervision, watch and ward for six months @ Rs. 600 p.m.	:	3,600.00	13.76
* Depreciation on implements and equipments	:	100.00	0.38
* Interest on working capital @ 12% p.a. for six months	:	1,475.00	5.64
Total Cost	:	26,158.00	100.00
Cost per seedling raised	:	30.52 paise	

Major Cost Components	*% total*
(i) Labour	51.50
(ii) Poly bags	39.31

TABLE 4.3: Cost of seedling raising at nurseries — *Casuarina equisetifolia* sp.

Species	:	*Casuarina equisetifolia*	
Method of raising	:	Seed bed and polybag containers	
Bed size	:	10m × 1.2m or 12 m^2	
Number of beds	:	20	
Total beds area	:	240 sq. metres	
Distance between seedlings	:	7.5cm × 7.5cm or 0.0056 m^2	
Space occupied by one plant	:	$\frac{0.0056}{2}$ or 0.0028 m^2	
Number of plants in 240 sq.m	:	$\frac{240}{(0.0028)}$ = 85700	
Seed germination rate	:	65 per cent	
Mortality rate in beds	:	10 per cent	
Culling loss	:	15 per cent	
Total seeds required	:	$\frac{85,700}{0.65 \times .9 \times .85}$ = 132,000	
Number of seeds per kilogram	:	60,000 — 80,000	
Quantity of seed required	:	Two kg	
Seed rate	:	Rs. 100 per kg	
COST INVOLVED	:	Rs.	Percentage
* Seed value for 2 kg	:	200.00	0.83
* Seed transportation	:	25.00	0.10
* Seed treatment	:	25.00	0.10
* Labour required for bed preparation and sowing/broadcasting @ one bed per day per male worker with an average wage rate for Rs. 20 per day	:	400.00	1.66
* Organic manure for beds — 2 cart loads @ Rs. 45 per cart load	:	90.00	0.37

(*Contd.*)

* Coarse sand for beds — 2 cart loads @ Rs. 10 per cart load	:	20.00	0.08
* Irrigation the beds for 15 days by female labour @ Rs. 10 per day	:	150.00	0.62
* Value of poly bags @ 12 paise per bag (85,700 × 0.12)	:	10,284.00	42.79
* Organic manure required for bag filing @ 10,000 bags per cart load	:	382.00	1.59
* Coarse sand required for bag filling @ 10,000 bags per cart load	:	85.00	0.35
* Labour required for bag filling including sieving to remove pebbles @ 200 bags per day by female labour	:	4,285.00	17.83
* Pesticides	:	100.00	0.42
* Transplanting of seedlings into poly bags @ 200 plants per day by female worker	:	4,285.00	17.83
* Irrigation and weeding the poly bags for 30 days by female labour	:	300.00	1.23
* Supervision, watch and ward for four months @ Rs. 600 p.m.	:	2,400.00	9.98
* Depreciation on implements and equipments	:	75.00	0.31
* Interest on working capital @ 12% p.a. for four months	:	929.00	3.86
Total Cost	:	24,036.00	100.00
Cost per seedling raised	:	28.04 paise	

Major Cost Components	*% to total*
(i) Labour	49.17
(ii) Poly bags	42.79

TABLE 4.4: Cost of seedlings, raising at nurseries — *Dulbergia sissoo* sp.

Species	:	*Dulbergia sissoo*
Method of raising	:	Seed bed and polybag containers
Bed size	:	10m × 1.2m or 12m²
Number of beds	:	20
Total beds area	:	240 sq. metres
Distance between seedlings	:	7.5cm × 7.5cm or 0.0056m²
Space occupied by one plant	:	$\frac{0.0056}{2}$ or 0.0028m²
Number of plants in 240 sq.m	:	$\frac{240}{(0.0028)} = 85,700$
Seed germination rate	:	90 — 100% or 95% average
Mortality rate in beds	:	10%

(*Contd.*)

Culling loss	:	15%
Total seeds required	:	$\frac{85,700}{0.65 \times 0.9 \times 0.9} = 111,371$
Number of seeds per kilogram	:	53,000
Quantity of seed required	:	Two kg
Seed rate	:	Rs. 50 per kg

COST INVOLVED		Rs.	Percentage
* Seed value for 2 kgs	:	100.00	0.42
* Seed transportation	:	25.00	0.10
* Seed treatment	:	25.00	0.10
* Labour required for bed preparation and sowing/broadcasting @ one bed per day per male worker with an average wage rate for Rs. 20 per day	:	400.00	1.67
* Organic manure for beds — 2 cart loads @ Rs. 45 per cart load	:	90.00	0.38
* Coarse sand for beds — 2 cart loads @ Rs. 10 per cart load	:	20.00	0.08
* Irrigation the beds for 15 days by female labour @ Rs. 10 per day	:	150.00	0.63
* Value of poly bags @ 12 paise per bag (85,700 × 12)	:	10,284.00	40.93
* Organic manure required for bag filing @ 10,000 bags per cart load	:	382.00	1.59
* Coarse sand required for bag filling @ 10,000 bags per cart load	:	85.00	0.35
* Labour required for bag filling including sieving to remove pebbles @ 200 bags per day by female labour	:	4,285.00	17.89
* Pesticides	:	100.00	0.42
* Transplanting of seedlings into poly bags @ 200 plants per day by female worker	:	4,285.00	17.89
* Irrigation and weeding the poly bags for 30 days by female labour	:	300.00	1.25
* Supervision, watch and ward for four months @ Rs. 600 p.m.	:	2,400.00	10.00
* Depreciation on implements and equipments	:	75.00	0.31
* Interest on working capital @ 12% p.a. for four months	:	919.00	3.84
Total Cost	:	23,954.00	100.00
Cost per seedling raised	:	27.95 paise	

Major Cost Components	*% to total*
(i) Labour	49.33
(ii) Poly bags	42.93

TABLE 4.5: Cost of seedling raising at nurseries — *Cassia siamea* sp.

Species	:	*Cassia siamea*	
Method of raising	:	Seed bed and polybag containers	
Bed size	:	10m × 1.2m or 12m²	
Number of beds	:	20	
Total beds area	:	240 sq. metre	
Distance between seedlings	:	7.5cm × 7.5cm or 0.0056m²	
Space occupied by one plant	:	$\frac{0.0056}{2}$ or 0.0028m²	
Number of plants in 240 sq.m	:	$\frac{240}{(0.0028)}$ = 85,700	
Seed germination rate	:	80 — 90% or 85% average	
Mortality rate in beds	:	10 per cent	
Culling loss	:	15 per cent	
Total seeds required	:	$\frac{85,700}{0.85 \times 0.9 \times 0.85}$ = 1,31,805	
Number of seeds per kilogram	:	37,000	
Quantity of seed required	:	3.56 kg	
Seed rate	:	Rs. 80 per kg	
COST INVOLVED	:	Rs.	Percentage
* Seed value for 3.56 kgs	:	285.00	0.48
* Seed transportation	:	50.00	0.17
* Seed treatment	:	50.00	0.17
* Labour required for bed preparation and sowing/broadcasting @ one bed per day per male worker at the wage rate Rs. 20 per day	:	400.00	1.37
* Organic manure for beds — 2 cart loads @ Rs. 45 per cart load	:	90.00	0.31
* Coarse sand for beds — 2 cart loads @ Rs. 10 per cart load	:	20.00	0.07
* Irrigation the beds for 30 days by female labour @ Rs. 10 per day	:	300.00	1.03
* Value of poly bags @ 12 paise per bag (85,700 × 0.12)	:	10,284.00	35.27
* Organic manure required for bag filling @ 10,000 bags per cart load	:	382.00	1.31
* Coarse sand required for bag filling @ 10,000 bags per cart load	:	85.00	0.29
* Labour required for bag filling including sieving to remove pebbles @ 200 bags per day by a female worker	:	4,285.00	14.69
* Pesticides	:	100.00	0.34
* Transplanting of seedlings into poly bags @ 200 plants per day by female workers	:	4,285.00	14.69

(Contd.)

		Rs.	Percentage
* Irrigation and weeding the poly bags for 60 days by fomalo labour	:	600.00	2.06
* Supervision, watch and ward for nine months @ Rs. 600 p.m.	:	5,400.00	18.52
* Depreciation on implements and equipments	:	150.00	0.51
* Interest on working capital @ 12% p.a. for four months	:	2,395.00	8.21
Total Cost	:	29,161.00	100.00
Cost per seedling raised	:	34.02 paise	

Major Cost Components	% to total
(i) Labour	52.36
(ii) Poly bags	35.27

TABLE 4.6: Cost of seedling raising at nurseries — *Acacia nilotica/Acacia tortilis* sp.

Species	:	*Acacia nilotica/Acacia tortilis*
Method of raising	:	Poly bag containers
Number of beds	:	20
Bed size	:	10m × 1.2m or 240m²
Spacing between seedlings	:	12cm × 12cm
Space required by one plant	:	.12 cm × .12 = 0.144m²
Number of plants in 240 m²	:	$\frac{240}{0.0144} = 16,666$
Seed germination rate	:	80 — 90 per cent (85%)
Mortality in begs	:	10 per cent
Culling loss	:	10 per cent
Total seeds required	:	$\frac{16,666}{0.85 \times .9 \times .9} = 24,206$
Number of seeds per kilogram	:	6,000 — 8,000 (7,000)
Quantity of seed required	:	3.45 kg
Seed rate	:	Rs. 60 per kg

COST INVOLVED		Rs.	Percentage
* Seed value for 3.45 kg	:	207.00	2.92
* Seed transportation	:	50.00	0.71
* Seed treatment	:	50.00	0.71
* Organic manure for bag filling @ 10,000 bags per cart load — two cart loads @ Rs. 45 per cart	:	90.00	1.27
* Coarse sand required for bag filling @ 10,000 bags per cart lad — 2 cart loads @ Rs. 10 per cart load	:	20.00	0.28
* Value of poly bags @ 12 paise per bag (16666 × .12)	:	2,000.00	28.24

(Contd.)

* Labour required for bag filling (including sieving to remove the pebbles) @ 200 bags per day by a female worker wage rate Rs. 10 per day	:	833.00	11.76
* Labour required for dibbling the seeds into bags @ 500 bags per day by male workers-wage rate @ Rs. 20 per day	:	667.00	9.42
* Pesticides	:	100.00	1.41
* Irrigation and weeding of bags by female labour for 30 days	:	300.00	4.24
* Supervision, watch and ward for four months @ Rs. 600 per month	:	2,400.00	33.89
* Depreciation	:	75.00	1.06
* Interest on working capital @ 12% p.a. for four months	:	289.00	4.08
Total Cost	:	7,081.00	100.00
Cost per seedling raised	:	42.48 paise	

Major Cost Components	*% to total*
Labour	59.33
Poly bags	28.24

TABLE 4.7: Cost of seedling raising at nurseries — *Prosopis juliflora* sp.

Species	:	*Prosopis juliflora*	
Method of raising	:	Poly bag containers	
Number of beds	:	20	
Size of beds	:	10m × 1.2m or 240m^2	
Number of plants in 240 m^2	:	$\frac{240}{0.0144}$	= 16,666
Seed germination rate	:	60 — 80 per cent say 70 per cent	
Mortality rate in beds	:	10 per cent	
Culling loss	:	10 per cent	
Number of seeds needed	:	$\frac{16,666}{0.7 \times .9 \times .9}$	or 29,393 plants
Number of seeds per kilogram	:	5,000 — 6,000 say 5,500	
Quantity of seed needed	:	5.34 kg	
Seed rate	:	Rs. 90 per kg	

COST INVOLVED	:	Rs.	Percentage
* Seed value for 5.34 kg	:	480.00	6.54
* Seed transportation cost	:	50.00	0.68
* Seed treatment	:	50.00	0.68

(Contd.)

* Organic manure for bag filling @ 10,000 bags per cart load — two cart loads @ Rs. 45 each	:	90.00	1.23
* Coarse sand for bag filling @ 10,000 bags per cart load — 2 cart loads @ Rs. 10 each	:	20.00	0.27
* Cost of poly bags @ 12 paise per bag (16666 × 0.12)	:	2,000.00	27.23
* Labour required for bag filling (including sieving to remove the pebbles) @ 200 bags per day by a female worker wage rate Rs. 10 per day	:	833.00	11.34
* Labour required for debbling the seeds into bags @ 500 bags per day by male workers-wage rate @ Rs. 20 per day	:	667.00	9.08
* Pesticides	:	100.00	1.36
* Irrigation and weeding of bags by female labour for 30 days	:	300.00	4.08
* Supervision, watch and ward for four months @ Rs. 600 per month	:	2,400.00	32.68
* Depreciation	:	75.00	1.02
* Interest on working capital @ 12% per annum for four months	:	279.00	3.80
Total Cost	:	7,344.00	100.00
Cost per seedling raised	:	44.07 paise	

Major Cost Components	*% to total*
Labour	57.18
Poly bags	27.23

TABLE 4.8: Cost of seedling raising at nurseries — *Leucaena leucocephala* sp.

Species	:	*Leucaena leucocephala*
Method of raising	:	Poly bag containers
Number of beds	:	20
Size of beds	:	10m × 1.2m or 240m^2
Spacing between seedlings	:	12cm × 12cm or 0.0144m^2
Number of plants in 240 m^2	:	$\frac{240}{0.0144}$ = 16,666
Seed germination rate	:	50 — 60 per cent say 55 per cent
Mortality in begs	:	10 per cent
Culling loss	:	10 per cent
Number of seeds needed	:	$\frac{16,666}{0.55 \times .9 \times .9}$ or 37409 plants

(Contd.)

Number of seeds per kilogram	:	5,000 – 7,000	
Quantity of seed requirement	:	6.80 kg	
Seed rate	:	Rs. 150 per kg	
COST INVOLVED	:	Rs.	Percentage
* Seed value for 6.80 kg	:	1,020.00	12.90
* Seed transportation cost	:	50.00	0.63
* Seed treatment	:	50.00	0.63
* Organic manure for bag filling @ 10,000 bags per cart load — two cart loads @ Rs. 45 each	:	90.00	1.14
* Coarse sand for bag filling @ 10,000 bags per cart load — two cart loads @ Rs. 10 each	:	20.00	0.25
* Cost of poly bags @ 12 paise per bag (16666 × .12)	:	2,000.00	25.30
* Labour required for bag filling (including sieving to remove the pebbles) @ 200 bags per day by a female worker at a wage rate Rs. 10 per day	:	833.00	10.54
* Labour required for debbling the seeds into bags @ 500 bags per day by male worker at a wage @ Rs. 20 per day	:	667.00	8.44
* Pesticides	:	100.00	1.26
* Irrigation and weeding of bags by female labour for 30 days	:	300.00	3.79
* Supervision, watch and ward for four months @ Rs. 600 p.m.	:	2,400.00	30.36
* Depreciation	:	75.00	0.95
* Interest on working capital @ 12% per annum for four months	:	301.00	3.81
Total Cost	:	7,906.00	100.00
Cost per seedling raised	:	47.44 paise	

Major Cost Components	% to total
Labour	53.13
Poly bags	25.30
Seeds	12.90

TABLE 4.9: Cost of seedling raised at nurseries — *Albizia lebbeck* sp.

Species	:	*Albizia lebbeck*
Method of raising	:	Poly bag containers
Number of beds	:	20
Size of beds	:	10m × 1.2m or 240m^2

(Contd.)

Spacing between seedlings	:	12cm × 12cm or 0.0144m^2	
Number of plants in 240 m^2	:	$\frac{240}{0.0144}$ = 16,666	
Seed germination rate	:	60 — 90 per cent (AV. 77%)	
Mortality in bags	:	10 per cent	
Culling loss	:	10 per cent	
Number of seeds required	:	$\frac{16,666}{.77 \times .9 \times .9}$ = 26721	
Number of seeds per kilogram	:	8,000 to 13,000 say 10,500	
total seed required	:	2.54 kg	
Seed rate	:	Rs. 130 per kg	
COST INVOLVED	:	Rs.	Percentage
* Seed value for 2.54 kg	:	330.00	4.62
* Seed transportation cost	:	25.00	0.35
* Seed treatment	:	25.00	0.35
* Organic manure for bag filling @ 10,000 bags per cart load — two cart loads @ Rs. 45 each	:	90.00	1.26
* Coarse sand for bag filling @ 10,000 bags per cart load — two cart loads @ Rs. 10 per cart load	:	20.00	0.28
* Cost of poly bags @ 12 paise per bag (16666 × 0.12)	:	2,000.00	28.03
* Labour required for bag filling (including sieving to remove the pebbles) @ 200 bags per day by a female worker at the wage rate of Rs. 10 per day	:	833.00	11.67
* Labour required for dibbling the seeds into bags @ 500 bags per day by male worker at a wage @ Rs. 20 per day	:	667.00	9.35
* Pesticides	:	100.00	1.40
* Irrigation and weeding of bags by female labour for 30 days	:	300.00	4.20
* Supervision, watch and ward for four months @ Rs. 600 p.m.	:	2,400.00	33.63
* Depreciation	:	75.00	1.05
* Interest on working capital @ 12% per annum for four months	:	271.00	3.80
Total Cost	:	7,136.00	100.00
Cost per seedling raised	:	42.82 paise	

Major Cost Components	*% to total*
Labour	58.85
Poly bags	28.03

TABLE 4.10: Cost of seedling raised at nurseries — *Ziziphus mauritiana* sp.

Species	:	*Ziziphus mauritiana*
Method of raising	:	Poly bag containers
Number of beds	:	20
Size of beds	:	10m × 1.2m or 240m^2
Spacing between seedlings	:	12cm × 12cm or 0.0144m^2
Number of plants in 240 m^2	:	$\frac{240}{0.0144} = 16,666$
Seed germination rate	:	31 — 90 per cent (average 63%)
Mortality in bags	:	10 per cent
Culling loss	:	10 per cent
Number of seeds required	:	$\frac{16,666}{.63 \times .9 \times .9} = 32659$
Number of seeds per kilogram	:	1,240 — 1,760 say 1,500
Total seed required	:	22 kg
Seed rate	:	Rs. 80 per kg

COST INVOLVED		Rs.	Percentage
* Seed value for 22 kg	:	1,760.00	21.65
* Seed transportation cost	:	150.00	1.84
* Seed treatment	:	150.00	1.23
* Organic manure for bag filling @ 10,000 bags per cart load — two cart loads @ Rs. 45 each	:	90.00	1.10
* Coarse sand for bag filling @ 10,000 bags per cart load — two cart loads @ Rs. 10 per cart load	:	20.00	0.25
* Cost of poly bags @ 12 paise per bag (16666 × 0.12)	:	2,000.00	24.60
* Labour required for bag filling (including sieving to remove the pebbles) @ 200 bags per day by a female worker at wage rate of Rs. 10 per day	:	833.00	10.25
* Labour required for dibbling the seeds into bags @ 500 bags per day by male worker at a wage rate @ Rs. 20 per day	:	667.00	8.20
* Pesticides	:	100.00	1.23
* Irrigation and weeding of bags by female labour for 30 days	:	300.00	3.69
* Supervision, watch and ward for three months @ Rs. 600 p.m.	:	1,800.00	22.14
* Depreciation	:	75.00	0.92
* Interest on working capital @ 12%	:	235.00	2.89

(*Contd.*)

per annum for three months			
Total Cost	:	8,130.00	100.00
Cost per seedling raised	:	48.78 paise	

Major Cost Components	*% to total*
Labour	44.28
Poly bags	24.60
Seed	21.65

TABLE 4.11: Cost of seedling raised at nurseries — *Butea monosperma* sp.

Species	:	*Butea monosperma*	
Method of raising	:	Poly bag containers	
Number of beds	:	20	
Size of beds	:	10m × 1.2m or 240m^2	
Spacing between seedlings	:	12cm × 12cm or 0.0144m^2	
Number of plants in 240 m^2	:	$\frac{240}{0.0144}$ = 16,666	
Seed germination rate	:	75 to 100 per cent (average 87%)	
Mortality in bags	:	10 per cent	
Culling loss	:	10 per cent	
Number of seeds required	:	$\frac{16,666}{.87 \times .9 \times .9}$ = 23650	
Number of seeds per kilogram	:	9,850 — 14,800 say 12,325 average	
total seed required	:	2 kg	
Seed rate	:	Rs. 80 per kg	
COST INVOLVED	:	Rs.	Percentage
* Seed value for 2 kg	:	160.00	2.52
* Seed transportation cost	:	25.00	0.39
* Seed treatment	:	25.00	0.39
* Organic manure for bag filling @ 10,000 bags per cart load — two cart loads @ Rs. 45 each	:	90.00	1.42
* Coarse sand for bag filling @ 10,000 bags per cart load — two cart loads @ Rs. 10 per cart load	:	20.00	0.31
* Poly bags @ 12 paise per bag (16666 × 0.12)	:	2,000.00	31.48
* Labour required for bag filling (including sieving to remove the pebbles) @ 200 bags per day by a female worker at wage rate of Rs. 10 per day	:	833.00	13.11

(*Contd.*)

* Labour required for dibbling the seeds into bags @ 500 bags per day by male worker at a wage @ Rs. 20 per day	:	667.00	10.50
* Pesticides	:	100.00	1.57
* Irrigation and weeding of bags by female labour for 30 days	:	300.00	4.72
* Supervision, watch and ward for three months @ Rs. 600 p.m.	:	1,800.00	28.33
* Depreciation	:	75.00	1.18
* Interest on working capital @ 12% per annum for three months	:	183.00	2.88
Total Cost	:	6,353.00	100.00
Cost per seedling raised	:	38.12 paise	

Major Cost Components	% to total
Labour	56.66
Polybags	31.48

TABLE 4.12: Cost of seedling raised at nurseries — *Tamarindus indica* sp.

Species	:	*Tamarindus indica*
Method of raising	:	Poly bag containers
Number of beds	:	20
Size of beds	:	10m × 1.2m or 240m^2
Spacing between seedlings	:	12cm × 12cm or 0.0144m^2
Number of plants in 240 m^2	:	$\frac{240}{0.0144}$ = 16,666
Seed germination rate	:	66 per cent
Mortality in bags	:	10 per cent
Culling loss	:	10 per cent
Number of seeds required	:	$\frac{16,666}{0.66 \times .9 \times .9}$ = 31175
Number of seeds per kilogram	:	1800
total seed required	:	17.32 kg
Seed rate	:	Rs. 80 per kg

COSTS INVOLVED	:	Rs.	Percentage
* Seed value for 17.32 kg	:	1,385.00	17.89
* Seed transportation cost	:	150.00	1.94
* Seed treatment	:	150.00	1.29
* Organic manure for bag filling @ 10,000 bags per cart load — two cart loads @ Rs. 45 each	:	90.00	1.16

(Contd.)

* Coarse sand for bag filling @ 10,000 bags per cart load — two cart loads @ Rs. 10 per cart load	:	20.00	0.26
* Poly bags @ 12 paise per bag (16666 × 0.12)	:	2,000.00	25.83
* Labour required for bag filling (including sieving to remove the pebbles) @ 200 bags per day by a female worker at wage rate of Rs. 10 per day	:	833.00	10.76
* Labour required for dibbling the seeds into bags @ 500 bags per day by male worker at a wage @ Rs. 20 per day	:	667.00	8.61
* Pesticides	:	100.00	1.29
* Irrigation and weeding of bags by female labour for 30 days	:	300.00	3.87
* Supervision, watch and ward for three months @ Rs. 600 p.m.	:	1,800.00	23.25
* Depreciation	:	75.00	0.97
* Interest on working capital @ 12% per annum for three months	:	223.00	2.88
Total Cost	:	7,743.00	100.00
Cost per seedling raised	:	46.46 paise	

Major Cost Components	*% to total*
Labour	46.49
Poly bags	25.83
Seed	17.89

TABLE 4.13: Cost of seedling raised at nurseries — *Pithecellobium dulce* sp.

Species	:	*Pithecellobium dulce*
Method of raising	:	Poly bag containers
Size of beds/area	:	10m × 1.2m or 240m^2
Spacing between seedlings	:	12cm × 12cm or 0.014m^2
Number of plants in 240m^2	:	$\frac{240}{0.0144} = 16666$
Seed germination rate	:	45%
Mortality in bags	:	10%
Culling loss	:	10%
Number of seeds required	:	$\frac{16666}{45 \times .9 \times .9} = 45{,}723$
Number of seeds per Kg.	:	6700
Total seed required	:	6.82 kg
Seed rate	:	Rs. 50 per kg

(Contd.)

COST INVOLVED		Rs.	Percentage
* Seed value for 6.82 kg	:	341.00	4.74
* Seed transportation	:	50.00	0.69
* Seed treatment	:	50.00	0.69
* Organic manure for bag filling @ 10,000 bags per cart load — two cart loads @ Rs. 45 each	:	90.00	1.25
* Coarse sand for bag filling @ 10000 bags per cart load — two cart loads @ Rs. 10 each	:	20.00	0.28
* Cost of poly bags @ 12 paise each 16666 × .12	:	2,000.00	27.78
* Labour required for bag filling (inc. sieving to remove the pebbles) @ 200 bags per day by a female labour @ Rs. 10 per day	:	833.00	11.57
* Labour required for dibbling the seeds into bags @ 500 bags per day by male labour @ Rs. 20 per day	:	667.00	9.26
* Pesticides	:	100.00	1.39
* Irrigation and weeding of bags by female labour for 30 days	:	300.00	4.17
* Supervision, watch & ward for 4 months @ Rs. 600.00 p.m.	:	2,400.00	33.33
* Depreciation	:	75.00	1.04
* Interest on working capital @ 12% per annum for 4 months	:	274.00	3.80
Total Cost	:	7,200.00	100.00
Cost per seedling raised	:	43.20 paise	

Major cost component	*% to total*
Labour	58.33
Poly bags	27.78

TABLE 4.14: Cost of seedling raised at nurseries — *Terminalia arjuna* sp.

Species	:	*Terminalia arjuna*
Method of raising	:	Poly bag containers
Number of beds	:	20
Size of beds/area	:	10m × 12m or 240m²
Spacing between seedling	:	12cm × 12cm or 0.144m²

(Contd.)

Number of plants in 240m²	:	$\frac{240}{0.0144} = 16666$	
Seed germination rate	:	50 — 60 per cent say 55%	
Mortality in bags	:	10 per cent	
Culling loss	:	10 per cent	
Number of seeds required	:	$\frac{16666}{.55 \times .9 \times .9} = 37409$	
Number of seeds per kg	:	775	
Total seed required	:	48.27 kg	
Seed rate	:	Rs. 60 per kg	
COST INVOLVED		RS.	Percentage
* Seed value for 48.27 kg	:	2,896.00	30.97
* Seed transportation	:	200.00	2.14
* Seed treatment	:	100.00	1.07
* Organic manure for bag filling @ 1000 bags per cart load — two cart loads @ Rs. 45 each	:	90.00	0.96
* Coarse sand for bag filling @ 10000 bags per cart load — two cart loads @ Rs. 10 each.		20.00	0.21
* Cost of poly bags @ 12 paise each (16666 × 0.12)		2,000.0	21.39
* Labour required for bag filling (inc. sieving to remove the bebbles) @ 200 bags per day by a female labour @ Rs. 10 per day		833.00	8.91
* Labour required for dibbling the seeds into bags @ 500 bags per day by male labour @ Rs.20 per day	:	667.00	7.13
* Pesticides	:	100.00	1.07
* Irrigation and weeding of bags three months @ Rs. 600 per month	:	300.00	3.21
* Depreciation	:	75.00	0.80
* Interest on working capital @ 12% per annum for 3 months	:	270.00	2.89
Total Cost	:	9,351.00	100.00
Cost per seedling raised	:	56.11 paise	

Major cost component	*% to total*
Labour	38.50
Poly bags	21.39
Seed	30.97

TABLE 4.15: Cost of seedling raised at nurseries — *Azadirachta indica* sp.

Species	:	*Azadirachta indica*
Method of raising	:	Poly bag containers
Number of beds	:	20
Size of beds/area	:	10m × 1.2m or 240m^2
Spacing between seedling	:	12cm × 12cm or 0.0144m^2
Number of plants in 240m^2	:	$\frac{240}{0.0144}$ = 16,666
Seed germination rate	:	100 per cent
Mortality in bags	:	10 per cent
Culling loss	:	10 per cent
Number of seeds required	:	$\frac{16666}{1 \times .9 \times .9}$ = 20,575
Number of seeds per kg	:	3330
Total seed required	:	6.18 kg
Seed rate	:	Rs. 50 per kg

COST INVOLVED		Rs.	Percentage
* Seed value for 6.18 kg	:	309.00	5.49
* Seed transportation	:	50.00	0.89
* Seed treatment	:	50.00	0.89
* Organic manure for bag filling @ 10000 bags per cart load-two cart loads @ Rs.45 per each	:	90.00	1.60
* Coarse sand for bag filling @ 10000 bags per cart load — two cart loads @ Rs. 10 per each	:	20.00	0.35
* Cost of poly bags @ 12 paise each (16666 × 0.12)	:	2,000.00	35.54
* Labour required for bag filling (inc. sieving to remove the pebbles) @ 200 bags per day by a female labour at wage of Rs. 10 per day	:	833.00	14.80
* Labour required for dibbling the seeds into bags @ 500 bags per day by a male labour @ Rs. 20 per day	:	667.00	11.85
* Pesticides	:	100.00	1.78
* Irrigation & Weeding of bags by female labour for 15 days	:	150.00	2.66
* Supervision, watch & ward for two months @ Rs. 600 per month	:	1,200.00	21.32

(*Contd.*)

* Depreciation	:	50.00	0.89
* Interest on working capital @ 12% per annum for two months		109.00	1.94
Total Cost	:	5,628.00	100.00
Cost per seedling raised	:	33.77 paise	

Major cost component	*% to total*
Labour	50.63
Poly bags	35.54

It is clear from the foregoing tables that there are large variation in the cost of seedlings production at nursery level. The highest cost comes to *Terminalia arjuna* (Paise 56 per seedling) while the lowest for *Dalbergia sissoo* (paise 28 per seedling). Labour is the main component of cost expenditure and its share ranges between 38 per cent to 59 per cent for different species. Polythene bags constitute the second main item of cost expenditure and its share ranges between 21 per cent and 43 per cent of the total seedling production cost. These two items of cost as their ratio to total expenditure for the individual species have been shown in the Table 4.16.

TABLE 4.16: Share of Labour & polybags in total cost of seedling raised at nursery level

Species	Percentage to total cost		
	Labour	Polybags	Total
1. *Acacia nilotica/A.tortilis*	59.33	28.24	87.57
2. *Albizia lebbeck*	58.85	28.03	86.88
3. *Azadorachta indica*	50.63	35.54	86.17
4. *Butea monosperma*	56.66	31.48	88.14
5. *Cassia siamca*	52.36	35.27	87.63
6. *Casuarina equisetifolia*	49.17	42.79	91.96
7. *Dalbergia sissoo*	49.33	42.93	92.26
8. *Eucalyptus spp.*	51.50	39.31	90.81
9. *Leucaena leucocephala*	53.13	25.30	78.43
10. *Pithocellobium dulce*	58.33	27.78	86.11
11. *Prosopis juliflora*	57.18	27.23	84.41
12. *Temarindus indica*	46.49	25.83	72.32
13. *Terminalia arjuna*	38.50	21.39	59.89
14. *Ziziphus manuritiana*	44.28	24.60	68.88

Raising Fuelwood Plantations

For raising successful plantations, selection of suitable sites and choice of right species are very important. If the objective is to raise particular species, sites have to be selected that match the requirements of the chosen species. On the other hand if a particular site has to be planted up, the species have to be selected that would grow on the chosen site.

Planting is generally carried out either in the rains or the winters. Before actual planting, a number of preliminary steps are carried out like survey and demarcation of the area, fencing, preparation of pits or making of lines for sowing (clearing the area and ploughing if it is not an agricultural plot), arranging irrigation etc. These activities are carried out in a planned manner so that by the time actual planting is to be done, all the preliminary steps are completed. Below is the most common time table showing by which time each operation is completed.

(i) *Site Preparation*

Survey and demarcation is started one year in advance and is generally completed by September/October. It consists of preparing a map of the area where plantation is to be carried out showing the general features like the slope, depressions, if any, site for digging tubewell, (if irrigated plantations are to be raised), the total length of the perimeter over which fencing has to be erected or protection trench has to be dug, the likely layout of the irrigation channels etc.

Soil working is completed by the end of February. This generally consists of clearing the area of all unwanted growth, removing the stumps, burning all brushwood after removing utilisable wood, and throughly ploughing the land with a heavy tractor.

Once ploughing is completed, if the area is large, it is divided into smaller blocks and 3 m wide paths are laid out. The size of the blocks depends upon the actual area of the proposed plantation. Normally blocks of 10-15 hectare are satisfactory. If the land is sloping, the slope is marked and the irrigation channels are made accordingly. Once the area is prepared, ridges are made with the help of tractors.

Where tractor power is not available and ploughing is not possible, only pit digging is done at the spacing decided upon. Strings are used for aligning lines and stakes are put at the places where pits are to be dug. Where ridges are made, the pits of 45 cm by 45 cm are made on the ridges.

The pit sizes very but the most common size is 45 cm cube. The earth dug from the pit is put on the sides of the pit. It is allowed to weather in sun for three months or so. A week or two before rains start, the weathered soil is mixed with farmyard manure at the rate of 2 kg and anti-termite chemicals added to it. The soil is mixed properly and then it is put in the pit. This operation is completed well before the rains break.

(ii) *Planting*

Before actual planting, the plants are to be transported to the planting site. A margin of at least 20 per cent is made when ordering plants to account for the dying or damage in transplanting and planting. Care is exercised in transporting plants from the nurseries to the planting sites. In particular the following precautions are taken:

- — Plants selected are of about 1-2 m in height, straight and healthy.
- — The polypots are not tear away and so that the root system is not exposed or damaged in any way.
- — While transporting the plants are kept in a vertical position.
- — The plants are stored near the planting site is sunken beds in the shade of a tree or a hut and planted in the area as soon as possible. If there is likely to be delayed in planting the plants are irrigated in the morning and evening.

In planting the following precautions are taken:

- — The plants are never lifted by the collar or the system. They are lifted from the bottom with care so that the ball of earth is not disturbed or the roots in the polypots are not shaken.
- — From the filled pit only earth that accommodated the polypot or the ball of earth is removed and the polypot completely removed with care from the plant before it is put in the pit. In the case of ball of earth the grass tied around the plant is discarded before planting. While planting care is taken to see that the collar is in level with the surface of the planting area, the earth is put back in the pit and moderately pressed around the plant. After planting the pit is lightly watered.

- Planting is never done in a pit filled with water. If water has entered the pit it is drained off before the plant is put in.
- Planting is carried out after the first good shower and is completed by the middle of July (latest by July end). Late plantation results in loss of time for establishment of the plant and it is not able to take full advantage of the growing season. Any failures are supposed to be replanted by the month of August.

(iii) *Post-planting Care*

After planting is completed the plantation needs intensive care for the next four months or so. The following is a list of operations are carried out:

- First weeding is carried out after 15 – 20 days planting. Second weeding is done in September and the third in the month of February. The February weeding is combined with through hoeing and a little earth is also piled around the base of each plant. Hoeing is done with the first two weeding also.
- Irrigation is provided according to the climate and soil; however, the following irrigation cycle is generally followed:

September to March — One irrigation per month
April to May — Three irrigation per month
June — Two irrigations.

Further irrigation is needed if rains do not break in July, or are delayed.

(iv) *Application of Fertilizers*

In case of poor and infertile soils, chemical fertilisers are applied at the time of irrigation. This is done to each individual plant. A dose of 10 gm of urea is applied by digging a hole by a sharp pointed iron rod about 0.5 m away from the stem. The fertilizer is filled in this hole which is about 15-20 cm deep. The plantation is then irrigated. The first application is made in August, then September and the last in October. No further applications are made till the next season. Chemical fertilizers are harmful if applied in excess. As in the case of irrigation, the best guide to the need for fertilizers is provided by measuring the growth of the selected stem. If the growth rate is falling, it is a sign that watering and fertilisation are needed. The usual fertilisers are urea and NPK mixture.

(v) *Spacing*

Different species require different plant spacing for planting. The most common number of plants to be raised at different spacings have been calculated in Table 4.17. The number of plants under the high density forestry will depend on soil and management conditions and also the requirement of need based species.

TABLE 4.17: **Number of plants per hectare in different spacing models**

Spacing	No. of plants per hectare
0.5 × 0.5 m	40,000
0.8 × 0.8	15,625
0.5 × 1.0	20,000
1.0 × 1.0	10,000
1.0 × 1.5	6,667
1.5 × 1.5	4,444
1.0 × 2.0	5,000
1.5 × 2.0	3,333
2.0 × 2.0	2,500
2.0 × 2.5	2,000
2.5 × 2.5	1,600
2.5 × 3	1,333
3 × 3	1,111
2 × 3	1,667
4 × 4	675
5 × 5	400

Source: Irshad Khan (1987).

(vi) *Cost of Plantation Raising*

The growing of plantations is a lengthy process. It takes a number of years for a plant till it is available for its prime use. A very limited work has been done to calculate the unit cost of energy plantations. Since the subject has recently been getting importance it has to require sufficient time for data collection until the plantations are ready for disposal. Most of the energy plantations supported by DNES are newly ones and the recent drought conditions had adversely affected their growth. However, the limited available data, have separately been described in the next chapter.

Marketing of Fuelwood

Most rural dwellers and especially near the forest belts have always regarded fuelwood as a free good something which costs only the labour of carrying it from the forest to the hearth. But free energy, like free grazing is subject to the tragedy of the commons: an over stocked commons cannot supply all that is needed, and it is no one's interest to take loss. However, current fuelwood shortages are atleast beginning to make one important point clear : if fuelwood is to be continuously available within reasonable distance and at reasonable cost it must be planted, managed, harvested, distributed and sold.

Urban dwellers, on the other hand, have rarely regarded fuelwood as a free commodity. They have had to buy both fuelwood and charcoal in the market place. As supplies have become scarcer, and as wood and charcoal have had to be carried further, so prices have risen.

Over the next few years, the supply of rural fuelwood will become increasingly commercialised and the concept of fuelwood as a free good will disappear. Not only is this inevitable; it is desirable — in spite of the excessive profit which may be exacted by rapacious middleman. A properly organised system for the distribution and sale of fuelwood will do much to protect the rural poor from exploitation by the urban middle classes.

Various studies conducted in the country have shown the sale of fuelwood is often an important source of income for the rural poor and that it is usually the poorest — the landless and the jobless — who depend on selling fuelwood. Many of those who now-have to travel long distances to collect fuelwood do so not only to provide fuel for the home but also to provide a modest cash income as well.

Fuelwood Prices

On account of the fact that production of fuelwood has not been able to keep pace with the requirements, the prices of fuelwood during the last 25 years in India have shown an abnormally high increase. Table 4.18 gives the prices of fuelwood at a number of selected urban centres during the years 1960, 1977 and 1986 with an annual growth rate for the two mentioned periods.

TABLE 4.18: Prices of fuelwood in urban centres

Centre	Fuelwood Price (Rs. per tonne)			Annual growth rate 1960 to 1977 (%)	Annual growth rate 1977 to 1986 (%)
	1968	1977	1986		
(1)	(2)	(3)	(4)	(5)	(6)
Ahmedabad	90.00	306.00	740.00	7.46	10.31
Ajmer	91.00	320.00	825.00	7.68	11.09
Alleppy	42.00	200.00	700.00	9.62	11.94
Amritsar	80.00	290.00	700.00	7.87	10.28
Palghat	34.00	84.00	350.00	5.46	17.18
Bangalore	47.00	225.00	657.00	9.65	12.64
Bhavnagar	81.00	250.00	425.00	6.85	6.07
Bhilai	65.00	150.00	500.00	5.04	14.31
Bhilwara	92.00	250.00	550.00	6.06	9.16
Bhopal	55.00	180.00	666.00	7.22	15.65
Bombay	84.00	262.00	1232.00	8.97	14.58
Calcutta	93.00	275.00	1040.00	6.58	15.92
Chindwara	31.00	113.00	340.00	7.91	13.02
Chikmagalur	34.00	156.00	357.00	9.37	9.64
Coimbatore	73.00	240.00	750.00	7.25	13.39
Darjeeling	39.00	109.00	338.00	6.23	13.39
Delhi	101.00	400.00	1000.00	8.43	10.72
Goa	92.00	220.00	667.00	5.26	13.12
Gudur	69.00	157.00	500.00	4.95	13.74
Guntur	66.00	250.00	700.00	8.15	12.12
Gwalior	64.00	225.00	811.00	7.68	15.31
Howrah	90.00	289.00	1094.00	7.08	15.98
Hyderabad	66.00	243.00	667.00	7.96	11.87
Indore	57.00	258.00	700.00	9.29	11.73
Jaipur	79.00	298.00	669.00	8.12	9.40
Jalpaiguri	47.00	169.00	463.00	7.82	11.85
Jamshedpur	57.00	175.00	700.00	6.82	16.65
Kothagudem	50.00	100.00	240.00	4.16	10.22
Madras	85.00	283.00	728.00	7.33	11.07
Madurai	73.00	179.00	658.00	5.42	15.41
Monghyr	47.00	200.00	600.00	8.89	12.98
Nagpur	60.00	150.00	608.00	5.54	16.83
Rourkela	56.00	150.00	600.00	5.96	15.65
Sambalpur	39.00	146.00	541.00	8.07	15.66
Srinagar	35.00	161.00	272.00	9.39	6.00
Varanasi	60.00	272.00	883.00	9.29	13.98
Yamunagar	83.00	262.00	800.00	7.02	13.16
Average price per 37 urban Centre	65.05	218.84	650.35	7.35	12.87

Source: SSR Prasad, *et al*, (1988).

The data presented in table 4.18 denote that the high growth rate in the prices of fuelwood at the various studied urban centres have been observed and that especially for the period 1977-86. The change in indices for the same duration under different concerned items of cost have been shown in Table 4.19.

TABLE 4.19: Changes in price indices in 41 urban centres

(*Consumer Price Index — 1960 = 100*)

Particulars	1977	1980	1986
Consumer Price Index	327	403	640
Food Price Index	347	409	648
Fuel and Light Price Index			
Fuelwood Price Index	348	493	924
Ratio of Fuelwood to fuel and Light price index	1.112	1.130	1.14
Ratio of Fuelwood to Food Price Index	1.099	1.357	1.64
Ratio of Fuelwood to Consumer Price Index	1.161	1.381	1.66

Source: SSR Prasad *et al.* (1988).

It is clear from the indices given in Table 4.19 that prices of fuelwood have increased faster than the consumer items. The fuelwood price index has increased more than the wholesale price index, food price index and fuel and light index during the 1977-86, ten years period.

To mention, the per capita forest area in Haryana is the lowest in the country as compared to other States. Its 82.3 per cent of the total population is still residing in the village and hence very much dependent on fuelwood for their energy needs. An investigation on the fuelwood prices in Haryana (Mathur *et al.* 1984) shows that within ten years period i.e. from 1973 to 1982, the prices have trippled. *Acacia nilotica* and *Dalbergia sissoo* besides small quantities of miscellaneous trees are the main sources of fuelwood in the villages. During 1981 the *Acacia nilotica* prices went up from Rs. 34 to Rs. 37 per quintal while the rise for *Dalbergia sissoo* was from Rs. 29 to Rs. 40 per quintal. This case may not be of difference with the other States including having large areas under forest.

Marketing Systems

No doubt free competition in market does not exist in respect of fuclwood production. The market prices can usually be influenced by individual actions – the buyers and sellers being limited in number. Another factor which comes in way is hetrogeneous character of the product exchange in forest market. Really speaking there is a great difference in the amount of products viz., quality and case of access. There is virtually no monopoly in fuclwood products. Actually, there exists oligopoly in the local markets. There is more than one buyer or seller but not enough to effect the market price.

Since private forests are more or less absent in India, the production from the National forest has a great effect on price variations. Where there are some few buyers or sellers, they think that they can cause a change in the price in the market by their actions. Their tendency is to manipulate the situation to the best of their advantage. The case is of a pure monopoly. In case of oligopsony where few other buyers are active in the same area, the buyer will have to consider the effect of its actions as to how the other buyers will react.

Although there are no monopolistic trends in forestry in India but the forest department more or less monopolise the fuelwood production in the country. The foresters can sell their product from the forests at whatever price they like but generally at a much cheaper rate than anticipated in the market.

Various methods of fuelwood sales are adopted by forest departments. These can be divided as:

(i) *Lump Sum Sale*

Under the system the government is sure to get a fixed amount sale proceeds for a lot comparing an unknown quantity of wood. The forest department auctions the lot. Sale may be effected either directly or by tender. Afterwards the purchaser gets a licence or a permit for a period of time to extract the produce from a secondary product as a fuelwood after extracting logs etc. The exact amount of produce is known only on completion of extraction work.

(ii) *Payment on Out Turn*

The system covers the well known royalty system where the purchaser pays an agreed amount per unit of produce extracted. The payment of royalty is done on volume, weight or quantity of produce with guarantee of extraction of out-turn. The forest department notifies the area from where the produce is extracted within a specified period of time.

The intending purchaser apply for a licence or permit to extract material from the notified area. The forest department fix a fee for grant of a licence.

(iii) *Role of Head Loaders*

Besides the above sales, where large quantity of wood is involved in the transaction, small quantity of fuelwood products have been selling through headloaders during the past 20–25 years in the areas of Chota Nagpur (Bihar), Bankura and Midnapur (W.B.), Mirzapur (U.P.), many districts of M.P. and other forest belts of the country. The practice of headloaders is largely adopted by tribals and other people with little or no land. According to a study conducted at Xavier Institute (XISS), Ranchi, the headloading has become a major occupation of woman folk in these areas. In some of the villages almost 48 per cent of the households were engaged in headloading, but in majority of these villages, more than 20 per cent of the households were having headloading as their major occupation. The households either have little land or have uplands and wastelands mostly where agriculture is hardly remunerative. Most of the people belong to scheduled tribes and backward communities. The people collect fuelwood from the forests, carry them long distances some times 10 miles or more, partly by train and partly on foot and sell it in the nearest town for a livelihood. Female headloaders are mostly in the age group between 25 and 40 while majority of male headloaders are either below the age of 15 or above 40. Women at the best carry two bundles of fuelwood of 10 kg each and carry both the bundles on their head. One male headloader can carry four such bundles on *Bhar* two on each side of the shoulder. The headloader generally move in a group whether in the forest to collect fuelwood or in the market to sell it. They often spend the night at the railway station or some other public places and are exploited in matters of small illicit payments by the petty forest staff, railway running staff and the police. Each headloader household has to pay some money, to assure care free collection of fuelwood from forests. The whole process runs smoothly due to some invisible links and gentlemen's agreement between those who are involved.

Cost of Marketing of Fuelwood

Transportation is the most important factor in determining the cost of fuelwood. According to a study sponsored by the Food and Agriculture Organisation of the United Nations in the early 1980s, the price of fuelwood begins to approach that of oil when the distance transported is in the region of 400 km; and the charcoal becomes as expensive as oil at about 800 km. In practice, the distance cover which it is economic to transport fuelwood is considerably less. It rarely pays to use trucks to transport fuelwood over distances of more than 100 km. The production and marketing of charcoal is already a commercial business in most countries and one which is now likely to expand significantly because it is economic to transport charcoal over much greater distances than are viable for fuelwood (FAO 1985).

A study conducted by Manzoor Alam and others for fuelwood supply in the city of Hyderabad gives a following comparative cost (Table 4.20).

TABLE 4.20: Fuelwood comparative cost of transport by different means of transport around Hyderabad (1981)

Distance (km)	Cost of transport per tonne/km. in Rs.		
	Bullockcart	Motor truck	Railways
(1)	(2)	(3)	(4)
1 — 20	4.44	—	—
20 — 40	2.83	—	—
40 — 60	2.22	—	—
60 — 80	1.85	—	—
80 — 100	2.08	—	0.21
100 — 150	—	0.57	0.15
150 — 200	—	0.44	0.15
200 — 250	—	0.45	0.13
250 — 300	—	0.49	0.13
300 — 400	—	0.54	0.12
400 — 1200	—	0.43	0.11

Source: Manzoor Alam *et al.*, (1985).

Chatha *et al.* (1987) of the Economics Department of the Punjab Agricultural University conducted some farm surveys to calculate the cost of fuelwood marketing for the eucalyptus growers. The study summarises the following results:

The marketing of eucalyptus was not regulated under any act. The sales in the markets were affected in a most haphazard manner. In some markets, the price and other terms of trade were settled through haggling, in some auction was conducted for price settlement. In some of the markets, tender/*purchi* system was in vogue. Whatever was the mode of sale, the producers were exploited every where. There was no agency to look after the interests of the farmers.

The producer had to pay exorbitant market charges which varied a great deal from market to market. The various market charges payable by the producer were commission (2.5 to 5 per cent), brokerage (0.5 to 1.00 per cent) weighment charges (Rs.2 to Rs.6 per vehicle), unloading charges (Rs.0.25 to Rs.0.75 per quintal) deduction in weight locally known as *Kaat* (5 per cent) quality discount locally known as *batta* cash discount (up to 2 per cent) etc. The average charges are shown in Table 4.21.

TABLE 4.21: Average market charges in case of post-harvest sales in the market

Item of cost	Cost (Rs./quintal)	
1. Harvesting (cutting, loading etc. inclusive)	3.50	
2. Transportation (15 km)	4.00	
3. Octroi	2.00	
4. Weighing	0.10	
5. Unloading	0.50	
6. Deduction (*Kaat*)	5	kg/quintal
7. Commission	5	per cent of the sale proceeds

Source: I.S. Chatha *et al.*, (1987).

In case of pre-harvest sales outright bargains were affected invariably by all the farmers and no one undertook to pay anything for any service. For post-harvest sales, the farmers took their produce to the nearby city/town markets and the actual marketing costs per plant in case of border plantation which they had to bear have been shown in Table 4.22.

Punjab study on market costs may not differ with other States and for the various species grown for both the purpose i.e. fuel and timber. It may be mentioned that fuelwood in general have hiterto been usually grown in conjunction with the more valuable part of the tree namely the timber and the poles.

TABLE 4.22: Average marketing costs per eucalyptus plant of optimum size

Particulars	Costs (Rs.)	Percentage to total costs
1. Harvesting (cutting, loading etc. inclusive)	14.98	29.97
2. Transportation	12.25	24.51
3. Octroi	7.00	14.01
4. Weighing	0.35	0.70
5. Unloading	1.75	3.50
6. Commission	6.65	13.30
7. Deductions	7.00	14.01
Total	49.98	100.00

Source: I.S. Chatha *et al.* (1987).

5

ECONOMICS OF ENERGY PLANTATIONS: Some Case Studies

The case studies covered in the present chapter have made detailed use of quantitative and qualitative data derived from the projects under different agro-climatic regions of India. These studies have been carried out on the man-made forestry especially grown for the various fuelwood species.

Eucalyptus species

Eucalyptus is an Australian genus of about 700 species and sub-species, with numerous varieties and hybrids. The first Indian introduction on the genus dates back to around 1790, mainly as an ornamental tree,when a number of species of eucalyptus were planted in the Palace Garden in the Nandi Hills, near Bangalore. Regular trials were started in 1843 when Captain Cotton of the Madras Engineers successfully introduced blue gum (*E. globulus*) in the Nilgiri Hills of South India. The Nandi grown *E. tereticornis* commonly called Mysore hybrid or Mysore gum has been most commonly planted in varying climatic areas of the country. This species was first raised on a plantation scale in Karnataka in 1952. In Uttar Pradesh the large scale plantations of this species were taken up from 1962. Since then extensive plantations have been raised to meet the needs of fuelwood, small timber and pulp wood. In Punjab and Haryana where the area under forests in negligible, *E. tereticornis* has been planted in strips 3–6 rows deep along highways, canals and railway tracks. Some species of eucalyptus, *E. citriodora*, *E. globulus*, *E. grandis* and *E. camaldutensis* are widely grown in India. Of these *E. globulus* is a rapid grower, often considered to be the fastest growing tree in India. This was planted in Nilgiris to meet the demand for firewood but also became an important source of eucalyptus oil. *E. grandis* which was first introduced in Kerala in 1948, primarily for afforesting the grasslands of the high ranges, has emerged as the most important species for pulp-wood plantations in Kerala.

Chaturvedi (1983) has produced the expenditure and yields data of eucalyptus grown by the Uttar Pradesh forest department under the rainfed conditions. Accordingly, under these conditions the best yields have been obtained in mechanised plantations on deep fertile lands of the *Tarai* belt. The data based on 90,000 hectares plantations since 1962 show that the direct cost of production was about Rs. 240 per tonne or Rs. 144 per m^3. This is worked out after providing for two harvests, the first one from the main felling and the second one from the coppice crop and compound interest rate of 12 per cent. The average stumpage yield of these plantations are 23 tonnes ($38m^3$) to 28 tonnes ($46m^3$) per hectare, worked out on a rotation of 8 years. The yield of individual plantations have varied within wide limits. The estimated yields from felling coupes of 1982-83 varied from 0.2 tonne ($0.3m^3$) to 133 tonnes ($221m^3$) per hectare. Table 5.1 shows first year raising cost (during 1980-81), of mechanised plantations in Uttar Pradesh.

TABLE 5.1: Eucalyptus raising cost under mechanised plantations in U.P.

1	2	3
	Description of work	Rs./hectare
1.	Survey and demarcation	3.25
2.	Clearing of site	18.00
3.	Ploughing	93.00
4.	Harrowing (two)	36.00
5.	Ridging	23.25
6.	Nursery costs:	
	(i) Seed	5.70
	(ii) Preparation of nursery beds	134.00
	(iii) Pesticides	20.00
	(iv) Polythene bags: 21cm × 8cm × 150 gauge	134.00
	(v) Irrigation, weeding and other works	302.00
7.	Fencing:	
	(i) Cost of barbed wire 3 strands	580.00
	(ii) Erection charges	46.20
8.	Weeding (three)	168.00
9.	Maintenance of roads and paths	25.00
10.	Labour huts	28.00
11.	Provision of drinking water	9.00
12.	Sign boards	3.50
13.	Hoeing (one)	30.00
14.	Firelines: maintenance	28.10

(Contd.)

Table 5.1 Contd.

1	2	3
15.	Carriage of plants	15.00
16.	Plantation guard: one for every 200 hectares from July to March	10.00
17.	Cost of tractor parts & their maintenance	315.00
18.	Miscellaneous and unforeseen	15.00
	Total cost	Rs. 2000.00

Source: A.N. Chaturvedi (1983).

For the maintenance of coppice crops an expenditure of Rs. 1,500 per hectare has been provided. Major items include the cost of felling, planting in gaps, weeding, cultural operation, fire protection etc.

Eucalyptus have progressively been planted by a large number of farmers in the State of Gujarat. The farmers have planted the densely hybrid species under intensive fertilization and regular irrigation systems for a profitable fuelwood out-turn. At Vatva a spacing of 3 × 1 metres and at Kardej 60 cm × 60 cm has been experimented by the farmers. Vatva (near Ahmedabad) and Kardaj (near Bhavnagar) farmer's results have shown out-turn as 25 tonnes and 75 tonnes per hectare respectively i.e., a much high return what has been claimed by the Uttar Pradesh Forest Department.

Patel (1985) calculated the high density, high inputs eucalyptus plantations cost per hectare over a three years period on his farm at Kardej (Table 5.2).

The income and expenditure data from Table 5.2 show that total cost for a three years cycle of eucalyptus plantation comes to Rs 34,060. The net profit for the cycle period comes to Rs 1,65,940 per hectare i.e. about Rs 55,300 per hectare per annum.

Kalidasa Bhai and Ramesh Bhai Patels — the two brother farmers have a farm at Vatva in Ahmedabad district. The area of the farm is 78.9 hectares out of which a total of 64.75 hectare was progressively planted by them under eucalyptus plantations. The plantation started in 1973 at a spacing of 3 × 1 m with fertilisation and regular irrigation. The mean annual increment put on this farm by eucalyptus hybrid works out to 25 tonnes per hectare. Srivastava and Pant (1979) have given in Table 5.3 the account of expenditure and income for the Vatva farm.

TABLE 5.2: Cost and income of eucalyptus plantation at Kardej, Gujarat

(Per hectare)

Number of trees	25,000
Spacing	60cm × 60cm
Rate of survival	80 per cent
Period of cutting	3 years
	in Rs.
I. *Initial Cost of planting*	
1. Preparation of land	250.00
2. Castorcake 50 gm/plant	900.00
3. N:P:K: (12:32:16) 10gm/plant	750.00
4. B.H.C. 10 per cent 30 kg	60.00
5. Labour of Planting at 10 paise/plant	2,500.00
6. Irrigation: 20 per year @ Rs. 75/ha irrigation	4,500.00
II. *Labour*	600.00
7. Fertilisers: Urea 6.5 tons	13,000.00
8. Soil working: 5 times/year @ Rs. 100/ha	1,500.00
9. Cutting @ Rs. 0.50 per tree	10,000.00
Total cost in 3 years	34,060.00
III. *Income and profits*	
Sale@ Rs. 10 per tree	2,00,000.00
Net profit/ha	1,65,940.00
Net profit/ha/year	55,313.00

Source: V.J. Patel (1983).

TABLE 5.3: Income and expenditure of 65 hectare eucalyptus plantation under irrigated conditions at Vatva, Gujarat

(Rs. per hectare)

Year	Cost	Income
1973	5780	—
1974	1365	—
1975	1365	500
1976	1365	500
1977	1365	1125
1978	5336	44461
1979	1748	200
1980	4253	12900
1981	340	825
1982	4242	46084
Total	27,859	1,06,595

Source: Srivastava and Pant (1979).

The expenditure and income data for a ten-year period show that income is 3.83 times more than the expenditure. The annual cost per hectare comes to Rs 2,786 and the income to Rs 10,660 for a ten years period. The net income per hectare per annum comes to Rs 7,874 under the existing conditions of plantations. Singh (1988) has analysed the data for income and expenditure on farmer's eucalyptus plantations grown in Ambala, Jind, Karnal, Kurukshctra and Rohtak districts of Haryana. In all, 18 growers planted about 16 hectares under block plantations of eucalyptus. He explains establishment and recurring costs were counted for the total costs and harvesting does not include as the trees were sold standing. Table 5.4 gives expenditure and net returns data per hectare of plantation.

According to these figures the total cost per hectare per annum comes to comes Rs. 2,770 and the net income Rs. 11,444 for an eight-year production cycle.

TABLE 5.4: Average cost and returns from eucalyptus plantations in Haryana

Items	Rs./Hectare
1. Average number of plants	2032
2. Establishment cost:	
(i) Preparation of land	656
(ii) Layout	139
(iii) Digging and Filling of pits	709
(iv) Cost of seedlings	922
(v) Transportation cost of seeding	173
(vi) Planting cost	885
(vii) Manures and fertilizers	290
(viii) Plant protection	159
(ix) Miscellaneous	228
Total (i to ix)	4,131
3. Recurring/maintenance cost	
First year	3434
Second year	3434
Third year	2823
Average Fourth to eight year	2494
Total	22161
4. Total (2 + 3)	26,292
5. Total revenue received from sale of plants	1,17,848
6. Net revenue	91.556
7. Average price per plant	58

Source: H.S. Singh (1988).

Subabul (*Leuccaena leucocephala*)

Leuccaena leucocephala or *subabul* is a native to Mexico. More than 100 varieties of this species are known. These are classified into three general types:

(i) *The Hawaiian Type:* Shurbs or short trees up to 5m yield of forage and wood low but useful for re-vegetation of denuded and poor hillslopes in the tropices.

(ii) *Peru Type:* Medium to tall tress up to 15m short clean pole and extensive branches down the trunk; mainly forage varieties.

(iii) *The Salvador Type:* Tall tress up to 20m tree like, having large leaves and pods are thick branchless trunks, fast growing,high yielding, some selected cultivars of this type e.g. K-28 and K-67 are known as "Hawaiian Giants".

Subabul wood makes excellent fire-wood and charcoal. Its wood density and calorific values are exceptionally high for such a fast growing species. The wood is hard, strong, heavy, close-gained and easily workable for wide variety of carpentary purposes, make cheap constructional timber, poles are used as fence posts. Leaves, pods and seeds are nutritious, digestible and relished by cattle, sheep and goats. However, a toxic but feeding milch cattle on leaves is reported to increase the milk yields.

The species introduced to Pacific islands, Philippines, Indonesia, Papua New Guinea, Malaysia, India and East and West Africa are now pan-tropical.

In India, *Subabul* was introduced as early as 1931, for a demonstration under the Forest Research Institute, Dehradun. Recently under the social forestry programme, major species have extensively been distributed in the States of Gujarat, Maharashtra, Karnataka, Rajasthan and Tamil Nadu. In other parts of India like Madhya Pradesh, Andhra Pradesh, Uttar Pradesh, Bihar and Orissa these have been distributed to a limited extent.

Pune based voluntary organisation – Bhartiya Ago-Industries Foundation (BAIF) has been a pioneer for the experimental and extension of *Subabul* cultivation in India. BAIF has conducted a number of this important species trials under different climatic regions in the country. Relwani and Hegde of this organisation have carried out intensive work for more than 10 years at Urulikanchan under secure irrigation conditions. These researchers have also conducted several trials under unirrigated rainfed conditions at above 1250 mm, 1000 mm, 750 mm, and 500 mm rainfall locations throughout the country. K-8, K-28 and K-67 varieties have been tried under these trials. K-8 gives the best results and they claimed that K-636 is the new promising strain.

According to the results obtained under regular irrigation system, the yield after the end of four years, ranges between 150 to 200 tonnes per hectare. The subsequent harvests yield more biomass than the first harvest. In addition, as is claimed, two tonnes seed and several tonnes green fodder per hectare is produced during the years period. These results have been obtained when spacing was done 1 × 1 m and fertilizing with super-phosphate, muriate of potash and urea. Irrigation was provided once every 4 to 6 weeks from December to May.

Tables 5.5a to 5.5c give the cost of establishment, plantation and income per hectare of *subabul* cultivation under irrigation conditions.

TABLE 5.5a: Cost of establishment of *subabul* plantation at BAIF farm (Irrigated Plantation)

Particulars	Cost/ha(Rs.)
A. *Nursery*	
1. Seed 1.5 kg Hawaiian Giant K-8	50
2. 12000 Polythene base (20cm × 15cm)	700
3. Farm Yard manure 2.5 t	250
4. Collecting 5 t of soil	100
5. Fertilizer mixture (NPK) 150 kg	300
6. Labour on powdering soil and FYM,mixing with fertilizer and filling up bags	350
7. Rhizobium culture 100gm	15
8. Hot water treatment for seeds	10
9. Dibbling the seeds in bags and filling up gaps later	125
10. Labour and equipment for watering and weeding for 2 months	600
COST A :	2500
B. *Planting*	
1. Ploughing, harrowing, levelling and making irrigation channels	1000
2. Trench-cum-mound fence and planting agave etc.	500
3. Making 10,000 holes	700
4. 375 kg superphosphate + 75 kg muriate of potash +25 kg urea	
5. Transport of seedlings, transplanting and filling up gaps	500
COST B :	3200
Cost of establishment (A+B):	5700

Source: R.R. Relwani etc. (1981).

Table 5.5b: Total cost of *subabul* plantation at BAIF farm (irrigated plantation)

Sl. No.	Particulars	Yearwise cost (Rs.) per ha				Total
		1	2	3	4	
1.	Establishment	5700	—	—	—	5700
2.	Weeding	500	250	—	—	750
3.	Irrigation	575	575	575	575	2300
4.	Supervision	350	350	350	350	1400
5.	Labour on misc.	200	200	200	200	800
6.	Land rent	500	500	500	500	2000
7.	Felling of trees	—	—	—	2000	2000
	Total cost	7825	1875	1625	3625	14950
	Interest on capital @ 12.5%	734	1187	1555	1966	5442
	Cummulative total	8559	11621	14801	20392	20392

Note: Interest during the first year charged for 9 months and for 6 months on the expenses incurred during the subsequent years. Interest has been charged on the the cost of tree felling.

Source: R.R. Relwani *et al.*, (1981).

TABLE 5.5c: Income from four-year old *subabul* plantation at BAIF farm (irrigated plantation)

Particulars	Amount Rs./per ha
When sold as fuel wood:	
175 t wood at 25% moisture at Rs. 325/t	56,875
Expenses	20,392
Net income/ha/4 years	36,483
Net income/ha/year	9,120
When sold party as poles:	
5000poles of 3.75 — 4 m length at Rs. 15	75,000
50t wood from the left over of trees selected for poles at Rs. 275/t	13,750
80 t wood from other trees at Rs. 325/t	26,000
Total gross income	1,14,750
Expenses	20,392
Net income	94,358
Net income/ha/year	23,590
From Second and Subsequent coppice crops:	
Total cost of maintenance/4 years	10,315
Net income when sold as fuelwood/4 years	46,560
Net income as fuelwood/year	11,640
Net income when sold party as poles/4 years	1,04,435
Net income party as pole/year	26,109

Source: R.R. Relwani *et al.*, (1986).

It is clear from the figures given in Table 5.5a to 5.5c that the total cost of *subabul* plantation under secure irrigation comes to Rs. 20392 per hectare for a four-year cycle. Two types of net income has been received — purely as fuelwood which fetch up Rs. 9120 per hectare per year and secondly when sold party as poles (3.75 to 4.0 meter at Rs. 15 per pole) and remaining as fuelwood, the net income per hectare per year shot up to Rs. 23,590

Under rainfed conditions and at different rainfall intensity, the *subabul* was planted at various spacings highest the rainfall and closest the plants. The reported yield of fuelwood per hectare is 150 tonnes where rainfall is above 1250 mm, 125 tonnes at a rainfall 1000 mm, 110 tonnes at a rainfall 750 mm and the lowest as 95 tonnes at a rainfall of 500 mm per annum. The income and expenditure for *subabul* establishment under rainfed conditions is given in Table 5.6.

TABLE 5.6: Economics of establishing *subabul* under unirrigated conditions in different rainfall regions

Annual rainfall	More than 1250 mm	1000 mm	750 mm	500 mm
1	2	3	4	5
Spacing (m)	1×1	1×2	1×3	2×2
Trees/ha	10,000	5,000	3,033	2,500
Harvesting cycle (years)	4	5	6	7
Surviving trees/ha	9,000	4,500	3,000	2,250
Polypot Seedlings required/ha	12,000	6,000	4,000	3,000
Cost and income per hectare(Rs.):				
Poly pot seedlings	2,500	1,250	833	625
Field preparation	1,000	700	400	400
Trench-cum-mound fence with agave	500	500	100+	100+
			(*Prosopis juliflora live fence only*)	
Pits for planting (30cm³)	1,275	1,000	667	500
Fertilisers and application	500	250	167	125
Transport and transplanting of seedings	500	250	167	125
Digging Water tanks (12m × 6m × 1m) (To recycle rain water in first 2 years)	–	–	1,250	1,250

(*Contd.*)

TABLE 5.6 (*Contd.*)

1	2	3	4	5
Handwatering (21.4 times/year)	—	—	588	440
Weeding	750 (first 2yrs)	750 (first 2yrs)	250 (first year)	75 (first year)
Supervision	1.400	1,250	1,225	1,250
Land rent	2,000	1,750	1,800	1,750
Labour welfare etc.	800	750	150	—
Harvesting and collection of wood	2,000	1,000	667	500
Interest	5,081	4,878	5,768	6,076
Total cost/cycle	18,306	14,328	14,032	13,216
Yield of wood (t/ha)	150	124	110	95
Gross income ha/cycle @ Rs. 325/t fuelwood				
Net income/ha/hr	48,750	40,624	35,750	30,875
Net income when party sold as poles and remaining as fuel	22,611	10,199	5,745	3,795

Net profit of Rs. 5,000 per tonne of seed/cycle alongwith green loppings of fodder may be considered as bonus.

Source: R.R. Relwani *et al.*, (1986).

As the results of the Table 5.6 show the total and establishment cost under various rainfall intensity ranges between Rs. 13,216 and Rs. 18,306 for the four year cycle. The gross income per hectare per year also varies accordingly in the range of Rs. 2,523 and Rs. 7,611. The net income followed the same pattern — lowest to Rs. 3,795 per hectare per annum at 500mm rainfall and Rs. 22,611 per hectare at and above 1,250mm rainfall.

Prosopis juliflora (*Vilayati babul*)

Prosopis juliflora (*Vilayati Babul*) is a native to Central America and northern part of South America. It has been widely introduced in many countries of he arid world. The species is naturalised in Egypt and introduced to other countries of Africa — Senegal, Nigeria, Sudan etc Iraq, Kuwait, Vietnam, India, Sri Lanka and the Philippines are its new home in Asia.

The plant was brought to India by R.H. Beddome, then Conservator of forests, northern circle, Madras in 1877, and now occupies a fairly extensive area of semi-arid wastelands, ravines, *nullahas* etc. in the country. The species has spread out extensively in many parts e.g. Rajasthan, Gujarat, Maharashtra, Karnataka, Tamil Nadu, Harayana and Uttar Pradesh. Five varieties or forms are recognised in India, viz. Mexican, Australian, Argentinian, Peruvian and the Arid. The first two named are more common.

P. juliflora is a versatile multipurpose plant used as fuel, fodder, general utility timber, etc. It is excellent firewood and makes superior charcoal. It provides the bulk of fuel for local people in many areas, and is the cheapest and best urban fuel, collection of which provides income for the rural poor. Its heart wood is hard, heavy, strong, very durable, close grained, easy to work and furnish but does not take polish. The wood is used for fence posts, doors and windows frames, agricultural implements, tool handles, cheap furniture and other carpentary work. The pods are sweet, nutritious and valuable proteinaceous cattle food

The species is very fast growing, thorny, evergreen and has the ability to grow on very poor and dry soils and is one of the very few species which can come up even on saline and alkaline soils.

Extensively work has been done on the species in different parts of the country. In Gujarat, farmers have adopted *Prosopis* as a commercial plantation on the wastelands. Patel (1984) has reported that *Prosopis* plantation on 300 hectares gave a fuelwood yield of 31 tonnes per hectare per year in Bhavnagar. He also claimed that its yield in Vatva near Ahmedabad was an average to 25 tonnes per hectare per year. He specifies a high density plantation of 1.5m – 0.6m spacing.

The cost of cultivation and annual expenditure and income data for the 5th year onwards are given in Table 5.7a to Table 5.7b.

The initial cost till planting, is Rs. 3,000; half of this goes in raising the seedings into polypots. The cost for annual maintenance including fertilisation comes to Rs. 220 and total investment up to 4th year comes to Rs. 6,000 per hectare. The income starts to come in the fifth year and is calculated as Rs. 9,000 per hectare for fuelwood. In addition, Patel claims, Rs. 5,000 per hectare are earned through the sale of pods in the fifth year. Thus a total income of Rs. 14,000 per hectare is received. This gross income further rises during the next five years of the production cycle of *Prosopis juliflora*.

TABLE 5.7a: Cost of cultivation of *Prosopis juliflora* in Gujarat

	Expenditure in Rs. per hectare		
	Material	Labour	Total
Initial Expenditure			
Preparation of land	125	—	125
B.H.C. 10 per cent, 20kg	60	10	70
Raising seedlings at 15p/seedling (half is labour cost)	750	750	750
Labour for planting	—	2,000	2,000
Total	935	2,760	2,695
		Say	3,000
Annual expenditure			
Interculturing/soil working		100	100
Urea 40 kg	110	10	120
Total	110	110	220
Total expenditure for 4 years			
Establishment cost			3,000
Maintenance cost			1,000
Interest on investment at 12.5%			1,813
Total			5,813

Source: V.J. Patel (1984).

TABLE 5.7b: Annual expenditure and income on *Prosopis juliflora* from fifth year onwards in Gujarat

Year	Firewood in tonnes	Cost of cutting in Rs.*	Total expenditure in Rs.*	Income in Rs.*
5	30	3,000	4,000	9,000
6	36	3,600	4,600	10,800
7	42	4,200	5,200	12,600
8	48	4,800	5,800	14,400
9	54	5,400	6,400	16,200

* Includes Rs. 250 as yearly maintenance and Rs. 750 as annual interest on investment

** Considering the price of fire wood at Rs. 300 per tonne.

Source: V.J. Patel (1984).

Another farmer from Gujarat, Kalidasa Bhai Patel (1987), Who owns the Adarsh Farm also at Vatva near Ahmedabad, obtained an average yield of fuelwood from *Prosopis* of about 32 tonnes per acre per year. He raised a plantation of 100 acres on the commercial basis on a barren wasteland. Kalidasa Bhai Patel's income and expenditure account for the *Prosopis* plantation are given in Table 5.8.

During the five years of plantation growth the total expenditure comes to Rs. 3,31,700 against an income of Rs. 10,00,000 in the fifth year on a 100 acre farm. The income froms two components: fuelwood (Rs. 9,50,000) and pods (Rs. 5,000). A net profit of Rs. 1,550 per acre is thus calculated on the total expenditure (compounded to five years) and income received during the fifth year of plantation.

Poplars

Poplars occur naturally throughout the forests of the temperate and cold regions of the northern hemisphere. They are fast growing, moderate size of large trees. Australian and American section in Series like G-8, G-49, D-100, D-75, D-61, D-121, D-67 have been tried for plantation. Poplar wood is moderately soft and light and makes a good fuel. Its wood used as matchwood and light timber, used for fruit crates, water-torughts, cricket bats, turnery and artificial limbs. The growth of poplars is fairly recorded throughout Himalayas and Aka Hills of Assam, Jammu & Kashmir, Uttar Pradesh, Himachal Pradesh, Sikkim, West Bengal and Arunachal Pradesh.

Chaturvedi (1982) has carried out intensive cultivation with imported poplar species from U.S.A., Australia and Italy. The cultivation was more research-oriented trials including irrigation, fertilizers and carefully controlled ply to sanitary measures. He claims that the best results have been obtained in deep fertile soils with high water table areas in Nainital *tarai* belts. Poplar plantations under his guidance were raised over an area of about 1,335 hectares between 1965 and 1981 in the east, central and west *tarai* forest divisions of Uttar Pradesh. A plantation raised over and area of 20 hectares in Gangapur Patia during 1966 was auctioned on standing crop basis in 1981. This was raised on unirrigated soils with 14 × 16 ft. spacing. At the time of auction in January 1981, 172 trees per hectare were available. The analysis of expenditure and income is given in Table 5.9.

TABLE 5.8: **Income and expenditure from plantation of hundred acres of *Prosopis juliflora* near Vatva, Gujarat**

	Particulars	Expenditure in Rs.
1.	Labour expenses for digging 40,000 pits of 50 cm × 50cm mixing insecticide, fertilizers and filling pits	20,000
2.	B.H.C. powder 10% 2000 kg at Rs. 1.80/kg	3,600
3.	Chemical fertilizer, primary dose: DAP 5000 kg at Rs. 3.72/kg Urea 2500 kg at Rs. 2.46/kg	24,750
4.	Chemical fertilizer second dose after one month of plantation urea 2500 kg at Rs. 2.46/kg	6,150
5.	Seeds 50 kg at Rs. 15/kg	750
6.	Polythene bags 5" × 10" — 45,000 pcs (90 Kg) at 30/kg	2,700
7.	Farmyard manure two truck loads to be mixed with the soil used to fill the bags	600
8.	Weeding and irrigation expenses for four months after planting seeds in nursery	1,500
9.	Labour expenses of filling bags making beds and putting seeds in it	6,500
10.	Transportation expenses for transferring saplings from nursery to field	6,400
11.	Interculture expenses (to be done in Unettradus from the trees base). After one month of plantation and after the last rainfall	8,800
12.	Expenses for making channel along the field border and putting P.J. Seeds in it for fencing purpose	1,650
13.	Seed require for planting in the channel for fencing purpose 20 kg at Rs. 15/kg	300
14.	Fertilizer expenses and labour charges for putting this fertilizer for the trees on the border (fence)	1,400
15.	Interculture in the first year (twice)	5,000
16.	Two watchman Rs. 350/watchman/month for 5 years	42,000
17.	Cutting charges for approx. 3200 tons of wood at Rs. 60/ton	1,92,000
18.	Labour expenses for collecting 100 tons of P.J. Pods	7,500
	Total expenditure for five years	3,31,700
19.	P.J. Pods used for cattle feed 100 tons at Rs. 500/tons	50,000
20.	Firewood 3200 tons at Rs. 300/ton	9,660,000
	Total income	10,10,000
	Total expenditure	3,31,700
	Net profit from 100 acres	6,78,300
	Net Profit per acre per year	1,550

Source: Kalidas B. Patel (1987).

TABLE 5.9: Economics of Poplar plantations in Gangapur Patia, U.P.

Year	Main operation	Expenditure (Rs.)	Income Source	Income Revenue (Rs.)
1966	Soil working & Planting	8322.25	Lease money from agric.	6,400
1967	Beating up and Maintenance	3092.00		
1968	- do -	1866.42	—	—
1969	Maintenance	671.00	—	—
1970	-do-	215.00	—	—
1971	-do-	771.20	—	—
1972	Maintenance & running	4077.90	—	—
1973	Maintenance	318.40	—	—
1974	-do-	923.94	—	—
1977	—	—	-do-	6,400
1978	Maintenance	800.00	-do-	1,600
1981	—	—	Auction bid	2,72,000
Total amount compounded at 13% of the year 1981		1,01,840.00		3,24,771

Source: A.N. Chaturvedi (1982).

On the basis of these information, the total compounded figures for expenditure and income come to Rs. 10,184 and Rs. 2,72,000 respectively. Thus a net income of Rs. 1,70,160 is received on 20 hectare plantation. The net income per hectare per annum comes to Rs. 850 without any inter-cropping. This is based on a rotation of 10 years. However, it has been suggested that with intensive farming, irrigation and manuring a shorter rotation of 6–8 years can be adopted.

Chandra (1986), has calculated the cost and income on Poplar plantation in the *tarai* belt of Uttar Pradesh. He has obtained the results with the inter-cropping of poplars along with sugarcane, wheat, maize, potato, gram, mustard, soyabean, peas, fodder crops etc. Accordingly, he explains that there is no bad effect on the yields of these crops while inter-cropping poplar plantation. Tables 5.10 and 5.11 give the income and expenditure data for cultivating the poplar plantation.

TABLE 5.10: Per hectare expenditure of Poplar (G-3,G-48 or D-121) plantations in U.P. *Tarai*, at 5m × 5m (400 plants/ha) with intercropping

Year	Head of working Costs	Cost Rs.
1	2	3
I	1. Partial levelling of land	36
	2. One ploughing and two harrowing	500
	3. General layout of area	24
	4. Preparation of irrigation channel	350
	5. Digging of 400 pits, sized 15 × 90cm @ Rs. 0.50per pit	200
	6. Cost of Emissan and Aldrin	40
	7. 400 Poplar clones @ Rs. 12.50 per plant	5,000
	8. Extension charges @ Rs. 11/- per plant	4,400
	9. 2 quintal Superphosphate @ Rs. 125/qtl	250
	10. 10 Qtls F.Y.M. @ Rs. 19/- per qtl (including carriage,loading and unloading)	120
	11. Mixing of F.Y.M., Aldrin, Superphosphate & filling of pits	60
	12. 10 irrigations @ Rs. 60 irrigations	600
	13. 3 weedings (5 mandays will be required/weeding).	180
	Total	11,760
II	1. Replacement of 10% plants as casualties (includeing all other costs)	170
	2. Weeding and soil working 2 times; in 1st weeding 1 man will weed 40 plants in a day, for 2nd weeding 1 man will weed 50 plants in a day	216
	3. Training leader 1 man will attend 50 plants	96
	4. Horrowing 2 times @ Rs. 100 per harrowing	200
	5. Irrigation 5 times @ Rs. 60 irrigation	300
	6. Extension during IInd year @ Rs. 6 per tree	2,400
	Total	3,382
III	1. Tods (secateur and bamboo ladder etc.)	25
	2. Prunning/cutting back coleader of plants @ Rs. 0.50 per plant	200
	3. Irrigated 5 times @ Rs. 60 per irrigation	300
	4. 2 soil working around the plants @ 8 mandays required per working	192
	5. Urea @ 250 g per plant	
	6. Extension charges as 3rd year @ Rs. 5 per tree	2,024
	Total	2,951

(*Contd.*)

TABLE 5.10 (*Contd.*)

1	2	3
IV	1. 2 Soil working around the plants @ 8 mandays required per working	192
	2. 2 irrigation @ Rs. 60 per irrigation	120
	3. Urea 500 g per plant in doses	400
	4. Application of Urea, 2 mandays.	48
	5. Prunning/Debudding/Training leader @ Re. 1 per tree	
	6. Pesticides etc. applying thereof	100
	7. Maintenance of tools etc.	100
V	8. Extension charges @ Rs. 4 per tree	1600
	Total	2,960
VI	1. Extension charges @ Re. 1 above	400
VII	2. Expenses incurred on the arrangement making for sale of trees	500
	Total	900

Source: J.P. Chandra (1986).

TABLE 5.11: Benefits received from one hectare of Poplar (G-3, G-48 or D-121) Plantation in U.P. *Tarai* at 5m × 5m (400 plants/ha) with intercropping

Year	Head of benefits	Benefits (Rs.)
1	2	3
I	Net Return received by normal agricultural crop	5,000
II	Net Return received by growing agricultural crop	3,000
III	1. Net Return received by growing agricultural crop	2,500
	2. Firewood received by Pruning of Coleader approximately 5 quintals fire wood received @ Rs. 40/q	200
	Total 3 year	2,700
IV	1. Net Return received by growing cash crop while shade crop like turmeric is grown	2,000
	2. Approximately 5 quintal fireweed received by pruning or by cutting of Coleader	240
	Total	2,240

(*Contd.*)

TABLE 5.11 (*Contd.*)

1	2	3
V	1. Net Return received by growing cash crop	2,000
	2. Approximately 8 quintal firewood received by cutting of Coleader	320
	Total	2,320
VI	1. Net Return received by growing crop like turmeric	2,000
	2. Approximately 10 quintal fireweed received by pruning or by cutting of Coleader sale @ Rs. 40 per quintal	400
	Total	2,400
VII	1. Net Return received by growing cash crop turmeric is grown	2,000
VIII	1. Net Return received by growing cash crop	2,000
	2. On the basis of 85% survival 340 trees will survive. As per WIMCO's experience approximately 0.40m wood will be produced by 1 tree. Thus the total volumes will be 136m evaluated at the rate of Rs. 1250 per m the rate of poplar wood expected to be in 1992 onwards	1,70,000
	Total	1,72,000

Source: J.P. Chandra (1986).

Kamla Singh *et al.* (1986) have also conducted economic investigations on the cost of Poplar cultivation and estimated income under the *Tarai* belt of Uttar Pradesh. They have obtained the results with the planting of poplars clone G-3 at the Research Farm of Central Institute of Medical and Aromatic Plants (CIMAP), Regional Centre Pant Nagar, Distt. Nainital. The planting was done in 1981 in rows of 5m apart; plot to plot spacing was kept at 4m and intercropped with *Mentha arvensis*, an annual crop. In another set of trial, it was planted in single rows during 1978-83 along the field boundaries, roads and irrigation channels at 3m apart, with 2 kg FYM and 5 gm Aldrex powder in each pit and regular irrigation. Tables 5.12 and 5.13 show cost and income data on the two types of plantation.

Singh (1988) has calculated the income and cost data for poplar growers of three districts in Haryana. The data for 15 block plantations measuring 48 hectares were collected from Ambala. Jind and Kurukshetra districts by the Department of Farm Forestry, Haryana Agriculture University Hissar. He has calculated the establishment and recurring cost but harvesting was not included since the trees were sold standing.

TABLE 5.12: Economics of poplar plantations in agro-forestry under CIMAP, Pant Nagar conditions

No. of years	Cost of cultivation (Rs./ha)			Gross return (Rs./ha)			Net return (Rs./ha)		
	Intercrop	Poplar	Total	Intercrop*	Poplar (95% survival)	Total	Intercrop	Poplar	Total
1	10147	2180	12327	22645	—	22645	12498	(–) 2180	10318
2	10697	250	10947	21940	—	21940	11243	(–) 250	10993
3	10932	285	11217	28055	—	28055	17123	(–) 285	16838
4	10271	200	10471	31625	—	32635	21354	(–) 200	21154
5	11511	200	11711	15150	47500	62650	3639	47300	50939
	53558	3115	56673	119415	47500	166915	65857	44385	110242

* Value realised after sale of oil during the crop year.

Source: Kamla Singh *et al.* (1988).

TABLE 5.13: Performance of Poplar (G-3) along boundaries/roads/channels at CIMAP, Regional Centre, Pant Nagar

Age of Plant (Yr)	Height (m)	Diameter (cm)	Value* (Rs./tree)	Value/ha 136 trees 3m apart	Value of fire-wood received by pruning	Cost of cultivation	Net Return	
							Rs/ha	Rs/ha/y
3	13	20-25	85	11,560	200	693	11067	3689
4	15	20-30	135	18,360	440	957	17483	4370
5	16.5	30-35	200	27,200	720	1157	26763	5352
6	18.2	35-40	250	34,000	1120	1320	33800	5633
7	21.5	40-45	305	41,480	1320	1550	41250	5892

* Value is based on the basis of cost realised per tree from M/s WIMCO Ltd., Bareilly during January,1986.

Source: Kamla Singh *et al.* (1988).

The income/expenditure data show that per hectare per annum cost comes to Rs. 4226 while revenue comes to Rs. 37,399. The details of cost and income have given in Table 5.14.

TABLE 5.14: Average cost and return from Poplar plantations in Haryana

Items	Rs/Hectare
1. Average number of plants	833
2. Establishment cost	
(i) Preparation land	378
(ii) Lay out	104
(iii) Digging and filling of pits	373
(iv) Cost of seedings	1227
(v) Transportation of seedlings	148
(vi) Manures & fertilizers	388
(vii) Plant protection	139
(viii) Miscellaneous	118
Total (i to viii)	3011
3. Recurring/maintenance costs:	
First year	3998
Second year	3975
Third year	4064
Fourth year	3981
Average — fifth to eight year	3720
Total	30,798
4. Total (2 + 3)	33,809
5. Total revenue received from sale of plants	3,33,006
6. Net returns (5 – 4)	2,99,197
7. Average price per plant	399

Source: H.S. Singh (1988).

Acacia nilotica

Acacia is a native of Sind and tropical Africa. This is now regenerated and cultivated throughout India. Three different varieties which come true to seed are recognised (i) *Godi* (ii) *Vedini* and (iii) *Ramkanta*. It can grow in a variety of soils. The medium sized, deciduous or evergreen, spiny tree with moderate growth rate, reaches up to 10m high. Annual bio-mass yield varies from 4 to 10m³ per hectare with 15–20 years rotation.

Wood has 4800–4950 calorific value, is heavy, durable, resistant to termites and very good for fuel, charcoal, farm implements etc. The bark and pods are rich in tanin content and used in leather industry.

Singh (1988) has calculated the income and cost expenditure for *Acacia nilotica* grown by two growers in Rohtak district of Haryana. The *Acacia* was planted on the wastelands and sold off as standing trees. He has calculated the establishment and recurring expenditure for the tree plantations as mentioned in Table 5.15. According to these calculations the per hectare per annum cost comes to Rs. 570 while the net revenue comes to Rs. 5880 for a twelve year production cycle.

TABLE 5.15: Average cost and returns from *Acacia nilotica* plantation in Haryana

Items	Rs/Hectare
1. Average number of plants	1389
2. Establishment cost:	
(i) Preparation of land	658
(ii) Layout	180
(iii) Digging and filling of pits	462
(iv) Cost of seedlings	1695
(v) Transportation cost of seedlings	180
(vi) Planting cost	600
(vii) Manures and fertilizers	133
(viii) Miscellaneous	38
Total (i to viii)	3946
3. Recurring/maintenance cost:	
First year	672
Second year	614
Third year	610
Average-fourth to twelth year	550
Total	6,846
4. Total (2 + 3)	10,792
5. Total revenue received from sale of plants	81,360
6. Net returns (5 – 4)	70,568
7. Average price per plant	59

Source: H.S. Singh (1988).

Studies on Mixed Plantations

In quite a large number of areas the mixed or inter plantation practice is followed for raising fuelwood trees. Under several experimental trials conducted at various stations, the cost/income data for different species have been shown in the following pages.

Mathur *et al.* (1979) studied fuel and fodder species on waste lands of Doon Valley from the view point of their economic utilisation. The programme was initiated during 1959-60 with two fuelwood species namely *Dalbergia sissoo* and *Acacia catechu*, the main wood species of the region. The plantation was raised at four spacings viz. 4.55m × 4.55m, 9.15m × 9.15, 13.75m × 13.75 and 18.30m × 18.30m. Fodder species *of Chrysopogon fulvus* and *Eulaliopsis binata* were also interplanted with these fuelwood species.

Grasses were harvested every year. During 1968 (i.e. 9th year) the trees having original spacing of 4.45m × 4.45m were thinned. Root suckers of *sissoo* were removed at 5 yearly intervals. Final fellings were done during 1976.

Table 5.16 and 5.17 give cost and income account separately for the two species.

TABLE 5.16: Economics of *Acacia catechu* plantation in Doon Valley

(i) Initial establishment and annual maintenance cost with their accumulation after 17 years' plantations

Tree spacing (m)	Initial establishment cost in Rs./ha		Annual maintenance cost in Rs./ha		Total accumulation (Rs./ha)
	Initial establishment	Accumulation at the end	Annual maintenance	Accumulation at the end	
4.55 × 4.55	1000	5054	150	6082	11136
9.15 × 9.15	500	2780	100	4055	6835
13.75 × 13.75	450	2274	80	3244	5518
18.30 × 18.30	400	2022	65	2635	4657

(ii) Income from final felling, root suckers and thinning of trees

Tree spacing (m)	Income at the end			Total accumulated income (Rs./ha)
	Final felling	Root suckers	Thinning	
4.55 × 4.55	1970	315	628	2652
9.15 × 9.15	1140	—	—	1140
13.75 × 13.75	649	—	—	649
18.30 × 18.30	367	—	—	367

Source: H.N. Mathur etc. (1979).

TABLE 5.17: Economics of *Dalbergia sissoo* plantation in Doon valley

(i) Initial establishment and annual maintenance cost with their accumulation after 17 years' plantation

Tree spacing (m)	Initial establishment cost in Rs./ha		Annual maintenance cost in Rs./ha		Total accumulation (Rs./ha)
	Initial establishment	Accumulation at the end	Annual maintenance	Accumulation	
4.55 × 4.55	1000	5054	150	6082	11136
9.15 × 9.15	550	2780	100	4055	6835
13.75 × 13.75	450	2274	80	3244	5518
18.30 × 18.30	400	2022	65	2635	4657

(ii) Income from final felling, root suckers and thinning of trees

Tree spacing (m)	Income at the end (Rs./ha)			Total accumulated income
	Final felling	Root suckers	Thinning	
4.55 × 4.55	1714	315	628	2711
9.15 × 9.15	8369	315	—	8684
13.75 × 13.75	2323	315	—	2638
18.30 × 18.30	1960	315	—	2275

Source: H.N. Mathur *et al.* (1979).

Accordingly, the removal of *sissoo* root suckers at 5th, 10th and 15th years after establishment gave an income of Rs. 50 per hectare with a total income of Rs. 315 obtained during the 17 years of plantation. The ninth year thinning of closer spacing gave an income of Rs. 350 per hectare with an accumulation of Rs. 682 at the end of 17th year. The per hectare cost ranges between Rs. 4,657 and Rs. 11,136 for *sissoo* and Rs. 3,796 and Rs. 11,146 for *catechu*. The maximum net income for *sissoo* comes to a total of Rs 11,938 or Rs. 702 per hectare per year. For *catechu* these figures are Rs. 27,034 and Rs. 1,590 respectively with the inter cropping of forage crops.

Sondhi family (1984) owns a farm in Meerut District (Western Uttar Pradesh). The farm is located on a dry highly alkaline belt (pH 0.5) of the region where agriculture crops were not profitable to cultivate. In 1981 the family planted an area of 200 acres under

TABLE 5.18: Cost of planting for one hectare and per plant in barren land of Meerut district in U.P.

Sl. No.	Particulars	years (1)	(2)	(3)	(4)	(5)	Total (Rs.) (6)
1.	Site preparation 2400 man days/ha/2 day	42,000	—	—	—	—	42,000
2.	Alignments & Staking 80 mandays @ 15	1,200	1,200	1,200	—	—	3,600
3.	Cost of plants 45 paise per plant in cluding carriage (specify nursery cost) 20 paise, 25 cartage cost nursery transported from forest nursery to & fro distance being 50 km	5,400	—	—	—	—	5,400
4.	Plantation & Replanting 80 mandays/ha as one man puts about 150 plants @ 15	1,800	—	—	—	—	1,800
5.	Weeding, 120 @ 15 mandays ha including split dosage of fertilisers time weeding in a required for 10 times	1,200	1,200	1,200	—	—	3,600
6.	Cost of fertilisers at plant FYM i.e. 1000 g N. 20 g per plant, 30 g k.p.10 g per plant	21,000	9,760	9,760	—	—	40,520
7.	Insecticides 80 mandays/ha	1,200	1,200	1,200	—	—	3,600
8.	Fire protection 365 mandays 4 ha 365 days a year @ 50P.M.i.e. includes No.12	1,200	6,000	6,000	—	—	24,000
9.	Head tools etc. lump sum 300 drill @ 20 spads 200 Nos. @ 30	800	800	800	800	800	4,000
10.	Irrigation costs for 10 weeks a year @ 80 per time	1,200	1,200	1,200	—	—	3,600
11.	Miscellaneous costs 10 per plant	750	750	750	—	—	2,250
12.	Protection/Fencing cost	???					
		1,41,252	37,846	37 846	920	920	1,91,785

In five years the average cost comes to 13.20 per plant, per year.

Source: M. Sondhi (1984).

eucalyptus and subabul with intercropping of sugarcane. In the alternative of planting the plant density per hectare was 12,500 trees for both the species. A ninety per cent survival rate was recorded during the second year fertilizers, irrigation and weeding was done according to the specifications provided by the number of experts from various organisations. The total cost up to fifth year of plantation have been given in Table 5.18. During this period the farmer has only reported the income from sugarcane crop but claimed a very good growth of the plants — eucalyptus with average height of 7 metres and plant girth 30 centimetres; and for *subabul* 6 metres and 22 centimetres on an average.

Kalla *et al.* (1975) have calculated the cost and income data on four species for arid areas of north-western Rajasthan. The basic data were based on the trials conducted under silvicultural experiments at Central Research Farm, Jodhpur and Research Farm, Pali. Four tree species namely *Albizzia lebbek, Azadirachta indica, Prosopis juliflora* and *Acacia tortil* which were found fairly suitable for commercial production on degraded lands of the arid zone were planted in the above trials. The data are reported for the period of 1963-64 to 1973-74. Tables 5.19 and 5.20 give the cost and income values for the four species.

The study examines that the plantation of fuelwood species is a labour intensive cultivation. High labour cost was due to its use on preparation of site, soil working, planting, cultural operation and maintenance. The total plantation cost comes to Rs. 281 hectare per annum. This cost exceeds the total revenues for the three species which varies from Rs. 211 to Rs. 237. For *Acacia tortilis* the plantation was profitable i.e. income exceeding to the costs by Rs. 81 per hectare per year.

Rao (1987), has reported the expenditure for 200 hectare of plantations in the Kutch area of Gujarat State. The area was planted during 1986-87 with six species at a spacing 1.5 × 1.5m on the less irrigated and degraded soils at village Moti Sindhodi in Abdasa Taluka. The area was covered as under:

Eucalyptus	:	25 hectare
Prosopis juliflora	:	100 "
Acacia nilotika	:	25 "
Acacia tortilis	:	20 "
Lelucaene leucocephela	:	10 "
Casuarina equisatifolia	:	20 "

TABLE 5.19: Production cost per hectare of some selected trees in arid zone of Rajasthan

Items	Physical quantity	Price/Unit (Rs.)	Amount (Rs.)
A) *Fixed cost:*			
Fencing-thorn facing for 400 m	running metre	@Rs.0.58 running	232.00
1. Site preparation layout	40 mandays	Rs. 3.50/ man day	35.00
2. Soil working digging of 400 pits of 60cm.dia and 60cm depth at 5m spacing	67 mandays	Rs. 3.50/ man day	234.50
3. Transport of planting material 400 plants	400 plants	Rs. 0.10/ plant	40.00
4. Planting costs:			
(i) Labour costs	5.7 manday	Rs. 3.50/ man day	20.00
(ii) Material costs	400 plants	Rs. 0.10/ plant	40.00
5. Interest on fixed capital	@ 9 per cent per annum for 10 years		332.55
6. Total fixed costs			934.05
B) *Variable costs:*			
1. Cultural operations	30 man day	Rs. 3.50/ man day	105.00
2. Cost of insecticides and application:			
(i) Labour	10 manday	Rs. 50/ man day	35.00
(ii) Material costs			100.00
3. Miscellaneous watch and ward	57 manday	Rs. 3.50/ man day	20.00
4. Total variable costs for formation year			260.00
— Maintenance cost during 2nd year including 5 per cent replacement: of casualties and watch and felling at the end of 10th year	—	—	500.00
— Maintenance for 3rd year	—	—	250.00
— Maintenance costs of 400m fencing @ Rs. 0.15/metre Rs. 60 per year for 10 years	—	—	600.00
5. Total variable cost for 10 yrs. period	—	—	2022.50
6. Total cost/ha for 10 years	—	—	2956.55
7. Total cost/ha	—	—	295.65

Source: J.C. Kalla (1975).

TABLE 5.20: Value of gross production from selected trees in arid zone of Rajasthan

(*in Rs.*)

Years	*Albezzia lebbek*			*Azadirachta indica*			*Prosopis juliflora*			*Acacia tortils*		
	Fuel	Seed	Misc.	Fuel	Seed	Misc.	Fuel	Seed	Misc.	Fuel	Seed	Misc.
1st	—	—	—	—	—	—	—	—	—	—	—	—
2nd	—	—	—	—	—	—	—	—	—	—	—	—
3rd	—	—	20	—	—	20	—	—	20	—	—	20
4th	—	—	20	—	—	20	—	—	20	—	—	20
5th	—	176	20	—	100	20	—	80	20	—	—	20
6th	—	176	20	—	100	20	—	80	20	—	300	20
7th	—	176	20	—	100	20	—	80	20	—	300	20
8th	—	176	20	—	100	20	—	80	20	—	50	20
9th	—	176	20	—	100	20	—	80	20	—	60	20
10th	1156	176	20	1349	100	20	1599	80	29	2500	—	270
	1156	1056	160	1349	600	160	1599	480	160	2500	710	410
Total		2,472			2,109			2,239			3,620	
Per hectare yearly benefits		237.20			210.90			223.90			362.00	

Source J.C. Kalla (1975).

It is reported that during 1986, the rainfall was only 75mm and that too in light showers. The survival rate was 95 per cent. About 4500 plants per hectare were planted. The total expenditure is given in Table 5.21.

TABLE 5.21: Rates for plantation activities at Moti Sindhodi, Gujarat

Items	Rate/ha (Rs.)
(A) *Raising of nursery:*	
1. Clearing the site	12
2. Fencing around nursery	10
3. Digging of beds	35
4. Cost of seeds	13
5. Cost of soil and manure	250
6. Cost of poly pots	180
7. Cost of insecticides	30
8. Cost of implements	80
9. Filling of polypots with soil mixed with manure and arranging in beds	80
10. Sowing of seeds/transplanting seedlings in polypots	25
11. Watering polypots (Feb./March)	25
12. Land rent, water charges, etc.	30
	935
(B) *Land preparation:*	
1. Survey and demarcation	10
2. Plouging and levelling the site	700
3. Trench fencing	150
	860
(C) *First year plantation operations:*	
1. Maintenance of nursery from April to June	285
2. Cost of manure	600
3. Transportation of seedlings	450
4. Alignment and planting	1200
5. Preparation of field channels	500
6. Cost of insecticides	100
7. Watering (Oct. Feb. & March)	1000
8. Weeding, soil working etc.	965
	5100
(D) *Maintenance of one year old plantation:*	
1. Watering (April, May and June)	800
2. Soil working	700
	1500
(E) *Maintenance of two year old plantation:*	
1. Watering	600
2. Soil working	500
	1100
Total: (A) to (E)	9495

Source: K.S. Rao (1987).

According to the above details, the total cost of plantation raised for the first two years comes to Rs. 9,495 per hectare. This cost works out to as for nursery raising Rs. 935 per hectare, land preparation Rs. 860/ha, first year plantation operation Rs. 5,100/ha, maintenance of one year old plantation Rs. 1,500/ha and maintenance of two-year old plantation Rs. 1,100/ha.

6

UNIT COST AND BENEFIT-COST RATIOS IN ENERGY PLANTATIONS

The energy crises in India, fuelwood situation, wasteland areas and cost pertaining to energy plantations including the marketing and wood prices have been dealt in the foregoing chapters. This chapter will study the unit costs and returns for investment on the plantations. As has been seen, there are some limitations with the information due to lack of available data: both for the most promising species as well as distribution of wastelands according to the agro-climatical zones. Attempts have been made for a wider coverage on the geographical locations of these plantations.

Fuel wood plantations as detailed in this study have been carried out under the field trial experiments at various research institutes as well as for the commercial production on private farms under certain constraints. These plantations can be classified as :

I. 1. pure species plantations.
   2. pure species plantations with intercropping including grasses
   3. mixed species plantations with intercropping
   4. mixed species plantations without intercropping

II. 1. block plantations
   2. strip plantations
   3. various spacing plantations
   4. high density agro-forestry plantations

III. 1. arid and semi-arid zone plantations
   2. hilly tracts including temporate zone plantations
   3. plains including *Tarai* belt of Uttar Pradesh plantations
   4. ravine area plantations

IV. 1. rainfed plantations at various rainfall intensities
   2. secure irrigation plantations with intensive culture.

These above factors have affected the unit cost of plantations raised even for the same species. As will be seen the range of variations have been very wide. The data calculated for costs per hectare of plantations raised and benefit-cost ratios for various species area as follows:

Unit Cost of Plantations

The highest unit cost of plantation has been for eucalyptus at Sunderbag, Kardej, Bhavnagar district of Gujarat (Patel, 1983). It accounts for Rs. 11,353 per hectare. Patel has increased plant population per unit area under HDAF by 6-10 times compared to conventional farm forestry. Accordingly, 25000 eucalyptus plants were grown at a 60cm × 60cm spacing, with 80 per cent survival rate. The bio-mass was ready for cutting after three years. The cost under these conditions is increased due to fertilizing (caster cake 50gm/plant; NPK 10g/plant, BHC (10 per cent) 30 kg urea 6.5 tons) and 20 irrigations. This has increase in bio-mass 3–5 times that obtained from spacing of 2m × 2m commonly used in conventional farming. Patel points out that selective cutting can be started after 2 years 9 months and the continuous cycle of cutting and income, the first one-third of trees are cut in forth year followed by one-third every year. In the seventh year, trees first cut are ready for second cutting. This has not only increased the cost of plantation but the net income through fuelwood cultivation.

The high cost of eucalyptus plantations at Kardej is mainly attributed due to Patel's commercialisation of energy cultivation. Other species raised at his farm also have high cost of production. Besides eucalyptus he grows *Prosopis juliflora, Leucacna leucocephala, Techona grabdis* and *Melia azerdarach* under HDAF. And in all the cases unit cost of planting is very high. The *Prosopis juliflora* has an initial expenditure of Rs. 6,000 per hectare for the first four years. The annual expenditure comes to Rs. 5,200 from 5th to 9th year of production cycle in the range of Rs. 4,000 to Rs. 6,400 per annum (Patel, 1986). Accordingly, the per annum per hectare cost comes to Rs. 6,700 for the *Prosopis* plantations. The high returns in wood production are attributed through applying manures, chemical fertilizers and irrigation.

Prosopis juliflora planted on barren wastelands near Ahmedabad on commercial basis costed about Rs. 1,625 per hectare per annum on a five year production cycle (K.B. Patel, 1987), DAP, urea and BHC powder 10 per cent were applied to the pots and in fields during the plantations period. A second dose of fertilizers was also applied along with FYM. The plantation was at two times interculture. Under secure irrigation system and with heavy fertilizers, the unit cost for *eucalyptus* plantation on the same farm comes to Rs. 2,786 per hectare for a ten years production cycle. The intensive use of labour is further recognised by Patel.

Tarai belt of Uttar pradesh has deep alluvium with high fertility. The forests in this belt are the richest, not only in composition but also for their luxurient growth. The mechanised plantation of *eucalyptus* in this Tarai belt cost about Rs. 2,000 per hectare (Chaturvedi, 1983). The plantation does not have use of any manures and fertilizers but pesticides and irrigation was given. About one-third of the cost comprises for fencing alone. The cost for maintenance of coppice crops is placed as Rs. 1,500 per hectare.

Eucalyptus are widely been planted in the northern belt of the country – both as strip plantation and block plantation. In five districts of Haryana where climate ranges between tropical to semi-desertic its cost per hectare per annum on block plantation comes to Rs. 2,385 on a eight year production cycle (Singh 1988). These costs include both establishment and annual recurring and maintenance. Trees were given fertilizers and irrigation and plant protection services as required were provided. This does not include the harvesting cost.

Subabul has been experimented at the BAIF farms near Poona both under irrigation pattern and at various rainfall intensities. Under irrigated plantations where 2.5 tonnes FYM, 150kg NPK was applied in the nurseries, besides 375 kg superphosphate, 75 kg muriate of potash, 25 kg urea in the planting holes with intensive irrigation and weeding practices the total cumulative cost comes to Rs. 20,392 per hectare. This accounts to Rs. 5,098 per hectare per year (Relwani and Hegde, 1981) for a four year production cycle.

The cost of production for subabul under different rainfall regions also has been calculated by the BAIF personnel (Relwani & Hegde 1986). At different spacings with the application of manures and fertilizers (NPK) and hand watering in low rainfall zones, the cost per hectare comes to Rs. 1,900 at 500mm rainfall, Rs. 2,338 at 750mm, Rs. 2,865 at 1000mm and Rs. 4,576 at 1250mm rainfall intensity. Close spacing (1 × lm) was done at 1250mm rainfall intensity while 2 × 2m was maintained at 500 mm rainfall. The unit cost as observed is linked with the production of fuelwood. In the high rainfall zone, cost of fuelwood production is high, this has resulted in high out put and vice-versa. This statement can be co-related with the production practices followed in Bhavnagar area where HDAF has given better results with high cost of production per unit area.

Poplars have been cultivated in the *Tarai* belt of Uttar Pradesh, Haryana and Punjab. The results available for *Tarai* and Haryana areas show that the per hectare cost ranges as Rs. 3,115 (Kamla Singh, 1988), Rs. 3,595 (Chandra, 1986) and Rs. 5092 (Chaturvedi, 1982) in the *Tarai* of Uttar Pradesh and Rs. 4226 (Singh, 1988) in parts of Haryana. Poplars have good demand in the area due to its readily available market. Western India Match Company (WIMCO), Bareilly is the prime user of poplars for its match factory. Poplars have been grown at these places for a rotation of 5 to 10 years production cycle. The major cost items for poplar consists irrigation, fertilizers and weeding. Block as well as strip plantations are practiced in the areas of cultivation.

Cost of plantation data available for *Acacia nilotica* in the semi-arid climate of Rohtak district, Haryana show as Rs. 900 per hectare (Singh, 1988) for a 12 years production cycle. The *A. Nilotica* was planted on a wasted land which was not suitable for cultivation any crop. About 1400 trees per hectare were planted, and FYM along with a dose of chemical fertilizers were applied to the plants.

There has been a practice in the conventional forestry to grow mixed fuelwood plantations. Several investigations have been carried out on these mixed plantations. To raise extra income and to utilise the soil cover, grasses are under planted with the fuelwood species. At different plant spacings *Acacia catechu* and *Dalbergia sissoo* were experimented in Doon Valley of Uttar Pradesh (Mathur *et al.* 1979). The initial establishment and annual maintenance cost for a 17 years production cycle for the two plantations varies from Rs. 4,657 to Rs. 11,136 per hectare. This calculated to Rs. 274 to Rs. 655 per hectare per annum. The cost is high on the close spacings (4.55m) and low on the wider plantation spacing (18.30 m × 18.30m).

The plant establishment in the hostile and inaccessible conditions of Chambal ravines, Kota district, Rajasthan is an expensive job. *Acacia nilotica* and *Prosopis juliflora* planted on a 20 years rotation cycle gives a cost of Rs. 642 per hectare per annum (Puri and Khybri, 1975).

The foregoing analysis amply shows that the variations in the unit cost have been mainly due to cultural practices in plantations, plant spacings and time gap – a sign of inflatory nature of prices. The data have been summarised in Tables 6.1 and 6.2. Under the high density agro-forestry concept as being adopted in parts of Gujarat and Maharashtra, the initial per hectare expenditure on fuelwood plantations ranges between Rs. 6,000 and Rs. 9,000. This expenditure as compared to plantations grown elsewhere in the country seems very high, particularly as wastelands are concerned. The initial establishment expenditure costs a lot to the growers especially on the development of nurseries. In cases where seedling cuttings are managed from outside, the initial expenditure is cut down. For example, the initial expenditure in case of poplars comes to about 9 per cent of the total cost. The range of variation of the initial cost of establishment is between 8.91 per cent and 36.56 per cent but no fixed trend is observed either with the duration of production cycle or the package of practices used for plantations under fuelwood species (Table 6.3.)

TABLE 6.1: Per hectare cost on irrigated fuelwood plantations

	Species	Plant spacing	Production Cycle (Yrs)	Cost per hectare per annum (Rs.)	Reporting year
1.	Eucalyptus	-	8	2000*	1983
2.	Eucalyptus	60cm × 60cm	7	11353	1985
3.	Eucalyptus	3m × 1m	10	2786	1982
4.	Eucalyptus	2023 plants/ha	8	3286	1988
5.	Subabul	1m × 1m	4	5098	1981
6.	Poplar	4m × 5m	7	5115	1988
7.	Poplar	5m × 5m	8	3596	1986
8.	Poplar	833 plants/ha	8	4226	1988
9.	*Acacia nilotica*	—	7	2611	1984
10.	Eucalyptus	—	7	2332	1984
11.	Eucalyptus	2m × 2m	10	810	1979

* This includes only first year raising cost.

Source: Chapter 5.

On a larger scale at All-India basis, the social forestry programmes have been taken up. A good number of these projects have emerged and are emerging with the help of the World Bank and foreign aid. Thus substantial capital is available for large scale afforestation of degraded lands with a view of developing fuel, fodder and timber resources and improving environmental qualities. The development of the projects have been done for aesthetic, social as well as for meeting environmental objectives. Economics is not a major consideration for these plantations. However, from the economic point of view, investments in connection with these projects are viable and profitable and from the social and ecological point of view the benefits are immense, as are claimed. The unit cost under these projects vary from State to State. Table 6.4 gives the details.

TABLE 6.2: Per hectare cost on rainfed fuelwood plantations

Species	Plant spacing	Production cycle (yrs)	Cost per hectare per annum (Rs.)	Reporting year
1. *Subabul*	1m × 1m	4	4,576	1986
2. - do -	1m × 2m	5	2,865	1986
3. - do -	1m × 3m	6	2,338	1986
4. - do -	2m × 2m	7	1,900	1986
5. *Prosopis juliflora*	1.5m × 0.6m	9	6,700	1986
6. - do -	400 Plants/acre	5	1,625	1987
7. Poplar	14 ft. × 16ft.	10	5,092	1982
8 *Acacia nilotica*	4m × 4m	20	642	1975
9. - do-	1389 plants per ha	12	899	1988
10. *Acacia catechu*	4.55m × 4.55m	17	655	1979
11. -do -	9.15m × 9.15m	17	402	1979
12. - do -	13.75 × 13.75m	17	324	1979
13. -do -	18.30m × 18.30m	17	274	1979
14. *Dalbergia sissoo*	4.55m × 4.55m	17	655	1979
15. - do -	9.15m × 9.15m	17	402	1979
16. -do-	13.75m × 13.75m	17	324	1979
17. - do -	18.30m × 18.30m	17	274	1979
18. *Acacia tortilis*				
19. *Albizia lebbek*	—	10	595	1975
20. *Prospopis juliflora*				
21. *A. Indica*				
22. *Acacia nilotica*	4m × 4m	15	647	1982
23. *Acacia catechu*	—	17	400	1982
24. *Dalbergia sissoo*				
25. *Acacia nilotica*	4m × 4m	1975	1979	1979
26. *Prosopis juliflora*				
27. *Eucalyptus*				
28. *Prosopis juliflora*				
29. *Acacia nilotica*				
30. *Acacia tortilis*	1.5m × 1.5m	—	9,465*	1987
31. *Subabul*				
32. *Casuarina equisatifolia*				

* This incudes only for the first two years.

Source: Chapter 5.

TABLE 6.3: Per hectare fuelwood plantation costs as for establishment and annual recurring

Species	Location	Production cycle (years)	Cost per hectare					
			Establishment		Total annual maintenance		Total cost	
			Rs.	%	Rs.	%	Rs.	%
1. *Eucalyptus*	Haryana	8	4131	15.71	22161	84.29	26292	100.00
2. *Eucalyptus*	Saurashtra	3	8960	26.31	25100	73.69	34060	100.00
3. *Eucalyptus*	Central Gujarat	4	5780	20.75	22079	79.25	27859	100.00
4. *Subabul*	South Maharashtra	4	5700	27.95	14692	72.05	20392	100.00
5. *Proscpis juliflora*	Saurashtra	9	3000	9.37	29000	90.63	32000	100.00
6. Poplars	Haryana	8	3011	8.91	30798	91.09	33809	100.00
7. *Acacia nilotica*	Haryana	12	3946	36.56	6846	63.44	10792	100.00
8. *Dalbergia sissoo/Acacia catechu*	Uttar Pradesh	17	1000	16.52	5054	83.48	6054	100.00
9. *Acacia nilotica/Prosopis juliflora*	Rajasthan	20	1603	15.06	9039	84.94	10642	100.00
10. *Acacia tortilis* *A. Indica* *A. lebbek* *P. juliflora*	Rajasthan	10	934	31.60	2022	68.40	2956	100.00
11. *Acacia nilotica*	Indo-Gangetic Plains	7	6416	35.11	11860	64.89	18276	100.00
12. *Eucalyptus*	-do -	7	6416	39.31	9906	60.69	16322	100.00

Source: Chapter 5.

TABLE 6.4: Per hectare cost under externally aided social forestry projects in India

State	Total Cost (million Rs.)	Coverage (Hectare)	Cost (Rs./ha)
I. *Multilateral*			
1. Uttar Pradesh (II phase)	1611.6	161950	9951
2. Gujarat (II Phase)	1296.5	313400	4137
3. Himachal Pradesh	572.9	112833	5077
4. Rajasthan	391.9	120800	3244
5. Haryana	333.3	82655	4032
6. Jammu & Kashmir	237.4	56310	4216
7. Karnataka	552.3	149500	3694
8. Kerala	599.1	86300	7023
9. West Bengal	348.7	117150	2976
II. *Bilateral*			
10. Andhra Pradesh	383.8	150725	2546
11. Maharashtra	564.0	81000	6963
12. Orissa	783.5	134400	5829
13. Bihar	538.5	112268	4797
14. Tamil Nadu	854.0	78380	10896

Source: NWDB and self calculations.

Among all the projects on social forestry (implementing or otherwise), Tamil Nadu has got the highest cost per unit of area, more than rupees ten thousand per hectare. The breakup of the total cost as shown in the appraisal project document for the foreign component contribution by SIDA is expected to 73 per cent on plantation, 15.55 per cent on staffing, 2,66 per cent on building etc., 3.73 per cent on vehicles and office equipment, tools, research, training, publicity, monitoring make together rest of the 5.06 per cent share in the State.

Cost-Benefit Ratios

The cost-benefit ratios based on the case studies in Chapter 5 and others unspecified in this report, have been carried out on the fuelwood plantations raised during the past 2-3 decades in India. The ratios conclude that plantations have yielded attractive financial returns along with improving the environmental situation of the country. The difference in package of practices for various fuelwood species under different wasteland categories result in sizable differences in benefit-cost ratios too. The vegetal productivity on these lands as said earlier are not characterised by high degree of economic resilience and viability. Yet these studies emphasised a different situation for the plantations.

The benefit-cost results of these studies as mentioned in Table 6.5 have an upper edge on the seasonal crops under the same agro-climatic conditions (Gupta and Gangwar, 1986; Gupta, 1979). The favourable ratios conclude that even on degraded lands planting of fuelwood species, the returns surpasses the benefits from any other fair market investment and particularly the farm business. Considering plantations a high investment high return business (V.J. Patel and K.B. Patel have established on in wood deficit areas) no field crop can compete with them even on best fertile soils of the country.

Poplars are recently introduced to the north Indian growers. The total area planted under poplar is estimated to about 2500 hectares (Chandra, 1986) and spread over in the States of U.P., Haryana and Punjab. The plantations raised in blocks as well as on field boundaries have paid higher returns. The trees have got a secure high demand market from WIMCo. and other industries using the soft wood. The high revenues and most favoured benefit-cost ratios where returns are over six times, the investment in Haryana supersede the all mentioned fuelwood species for plantations. Although the favourable ratios are attributed to the industrial demand of the wood but plant provides a sizable quantity of fuelwood. High return technologies for poplar growers as provided by WIMCo. besides assured marketing facilities and provision of bankable part of the inputs etc. have high value per tree and are realised almost in all the growing areas.

The benefit-cost ratios for eucalyptus are next to poplars. The high returned plantations of Gujarat and Maharashtra are more commercialised than rest of the plantations in the country. These plantations cater for wood scarcity areas and get better prices for their end uses. Also poles of the eucalyptus are being extensively used for construction purposes and hence fetch higher prices. These two factors, make the benefit-cost ratios more favourable to the growers.

Subabul has an additional income to be considered for high revenues for the growers. It is also a good fodder plant besides fuelwood and poles as a source of income.

On the other side of the story the fuelwood plantations in arid zones of Rajasthan and parts of Gujarat have paid negative or near to negative returns. Due to agro-climatic reasons, sandy and poorly soils of the area, the productivity of bio-mass from its germination till the tree grows to its prime use, are minimised. Intensive plantations on these soils are not feasible. The plant spacing at 5m × 5m also gives poor results. The tested species in this area like *A. indica, Prosopis juliflora, Albizia lebbek, Acacia nilotica, A. tortilis* have given low return to the investment. As is clear from the benefit-cost ratios, the plantations are not favourable to the growers as compared to other regions. Again, as has already been mentioned that due to large areas under deserts, the fuelwood plantations may not be profitable in these lands but there needs to be more plantations for striking the ecological balance.

Table 6.5 gives the benefit-cost ratios for fuelwood species planted over different parts of the country.

Table 6.5: Cost-benefit ratios on fuelwood production in wastelands

Sl. No.	Cost-benefit ratio	Species	Geographical/ zonal location	Constraints
1	2	3	4	5
I. *Negative returns*				
1.	1 : - 0.25	*Azadirachata indica*	Arid Zone western Rajasthan	Mixed plantations of four species, 10 years production cycle; income though fuel, seed tops & twigs; labour forms about 29% of total cost, Research plantations.
2.	1 : - 0.20	*Prosopis juliflora*	-do-	-do-
3.	1 : - 0.16	*Albizia lebbek*	-do-	-do-
II. *Returns less than 100 per cent*				
4.	1 : 0.29	*Acacia tortilis*	-do-	-do-
5.	1 : 0.32	*Acacia nilotica Zizyphus maurit-iana*	Saurashtra region Gujarat, arid area	Plant spacing 5m × 5m; non-irrigated arid soils; community plantations; cattle proof trench with *Prosopis juliflora;* 30 years product cycle.

(Contd.)

TABLE 6.5 (*Contd.*)

1	2	3	4	5
6.	1 : 0.76	*Acacia nilotica* *Acacia tortilis* *Prosopis julifora* *Azadirachata indica* *Acacia auriculi-formis*	Saurashtra region	-do- except cattle proof trench.
7.	1 : 0.78	*Prosopis juliflora*	North Gujarat Arid zone	Non-irrigated saline soils, plant spacing 5m × 5m, sparsely watered, 15 years production cycle, community plantations.
III. *Returns between 100 & 200 per cent*				
8.	1 : 1.04	*Dalbergia sissoo*	Doon Valley, Uttar Pradesh, Tropical moist forest region	Sandy loam soils, annual rainfall 1672 mm, plant spacing 4.55m × 4.55m, 17 years production cycle, stump planting, inter-cropped with *C. fulvus* grass, Research plantations.
9.	1 : 1.10	*Prosopis juliflora*	South Maharashtra dry region	On low production soils dry lands, 5 years production cycle.
10.	1 : 1.14	*Albizia lebbek* *Dalbergia sissoo* *Eucalyptus* *Mulberry*	North Gujarat Arid zone	Strip plantation, spacing 3m × 3m, irrigated soils, forest department plantations, inter cropped with napier grass, 10 years production cycle
11.	1 : 1.21	*Eucalyptus hybrid* *Casuarina equisatifolia* *mulberry, mango guava*	North Gujarat Arid Zone	Community plantations, partially irrigated, 600 trees per hectare, 30 years production cycle.
12.	1 : 1.22	*Eucalyptus hybrid*	Indo-Gangetic Plains	Alkali soils, use of Gypsum and FYM, community land plantations pH 10.5.

(*Contd.*)

TABLE 6.5 *(Contd.)*

1	2	3	4	5
13.	1 : 1.38	*Acacia nilotica*	Mahi ravines, Valsad, Gujarat	Fuel-cum-fodder plantations, plant spacing 4m × 4m, research plantations, 15 years production cycle.
14.	1 : 1.43	*Acacia catechu*	Doon valley, Uttar Pradesh, Tropical moist forest region	Plant spacing 9.15m × 9.15m, others like example 8.
15.	1 : 1.55	*Acacia nilotica* *Prosopis juliflora*	Chambal ravines Kota Rajasthan	Plant spacing 4m × 4m, 20 years production cycle, incoorporated with grasses *D. annulatum* *C. ciliaris:* experimental plantations.
16.	1 : 1.63	*Acacia nilotica*	Indo-Gangetic plains	Alkali soils, use of gypsum and FYM, community land plantations, pH 10.5.
17.	1 : 1.63	*Acacia catechu*	Doon valley, Uttar Pradesh, Tropical moist forest region	Plant spacing 13.75m × 13.75m others like example 8.
18.	1 : 1.79	*Acacia catechu*	Siwalik hills near Chandigarh Tropical moist region	Fuel-cum-fodder plantations, plant spacing 4m × 4m, research plantations, 17 years production cycle.
19.	1 : 1.80	*Acacia nilotica*	Chambal ravines Agra, Uttar Pradesh	Plant spacing 4m × 3m, planted with *C. ciliaris* grass, research plantations 15 years prodution cycle.
20.	1 : 1.86	Poplar	Uttar Pradesh *Tarai* region	Productive soils, irrigated plantations, 8 years production cycle, plant spacing 5m × 5m, intercropped with annuals & sugarcane, farmers plantations.

(Contd.)

TABLE 6.5 (*Contd.*)

1	2	3	4	5
21.	1 : 1.200	*Eucalyptus*	Semi-arid saline areas of Saurashtra region, Gujarat	Under high density agro-forestry system, intensive cultivation, plant spacing 60cm × 60cm, irrigated, fertilizing, 7 years production cycle, farmers plantation.
IV. *Returns between 200 and 300 per cent:*				
22.	1 : 2.02	*Acacia catechu*	Doon Valley, Uttar Pradesh Tropical moist forest region	Plant spacing 18.30m × 18.30m, others like example 8.
23.	1 : 2.18	*Dalbergia sissoo*	-do-	Plant spacing 13.75m × 13.75m others like example 8.
24.	1 : 2.25	*Prosopis juliflora*	Semi-arid, saline areas of Saurashtra region, Gujarat	Plant spacing 1.5m × 0.6m 5 years production cycle, farmers plantations.
25.	1 : 2.34	*Subabul*	At 500mm rain fall zone Maharashtra	Plant spacing 2m × 2m, normal fertilizing, hand watering, 7 years production cycle, institutional plantations.
26.	1 : 2.35	*Prosopis juliflora*	Semi-arid, saline areas of Saurashtra region, Gujarat	Six years production cycle, others like example 19.
27.	1 : 2.41	*Dalbergia sissoo*	Doon valley, Uttar Pradesh tropical moist forest region	Plant spacing 18.30m × 18.30m, others like examples 8.
28.	1 . 2,47	*Prosopis juliflora*	Semi-arid, saline areas of Saurashtra Gujarat	Production cycle 7 years other like example 19.
29.	1 : 2.48	*Prosopis juliflora*	-do-	8th year production cycle, other like 19
30.	1 : 2.53	*Prosopis juliflora*	-do-	9th year production cycle, other like 19.

(*Contd.*)

TABLE 6.3 (*Contd.*)

1	2	3	4	5
31.	1 : 2.55	*Subabul*	At 750mm rainfall Zone Maharashtra	Plant spacing 1m × 3m, normal fertilizing, hand watering, 6 year production cycle, farmers plantation.
32.	1 : 2.60	*Eucalyptus*	Semi-arid saline areas, Saurashtra	10 years productions cycle, others like example 16.
33.	1 : 2.60	*Subabul*	At 1250mm rainfall zone Maharashtra	Plant spacing 1m × 1m, fertilising harvesting cycle 4 years, farmers plantation.
34.	1 : 2.75	*Dalbergia sissoo*	Doon valley, Uttar Pradesh Tropical moist forest region	Plant spacing 9.15m × 9.15m others like example 8.
35.	1 : 2.75	*Prosopis juliflora*	South Maharashtra	Low production land, adequate moisture supply in soils, 5 years production cycle, farmers plantations.
36.	1 : 2.79	*Subabul*	South Maharashtra	Plant spacing 1m × 1m, with intensive cultivation, irrigation, fertilizing, weeding, entire product was sold as fuelwood.
37.	1 : 2.80	*Eucalyptus*	Semi-arid saline areas of Saurashtra Gujarat	12 year production cycle, others like 16.
38.	1 : 2.83	*Subabul*	At 1000 mm rainfall zone Maharashtra	Spacing 1m × 2m. harvesting cycle 6 years others like 20.
39.	1 : 2.93	*Acacia nilotica*	Semi-arid zone, Haryana	With manuring & fertilizing, 12 years production cycle, farmers plantations.
V. *Returns between 300 and 400 per cent*				
40.	1 : 3.04	*Prosopis juliflora*	Semi-arid, central Gujarat region	Intensive plantations, barren lands, use of FYM, 2 doses of chemical fertilizers, weeding, interculture, irrigation, farmers plantations, 50 cm × 50 cm spacing, 5 years production cycle.

(*Contd.*)

TABLE 6.5 *(Contd.)*

1	2	3	4	5
41.	1 : 3.10	*Eucalyptus*	Semi-arid, Saurashtra region of Gujarat	15 years production cycle, others like example 16.
42.	1 : 3.30	*Eucalyptus*	Semi-arid, Saurashtra region of Gujarat	18 years production cycle, others like 16.
43.	1 : 3.31	*Eucalyptus*	Moist tropics and semi-arid, Haryana	F.Y.M. & Chemical fertilizers use, irrigation, plant protection, farmers plantations.
44.	1 : 3.35	*Eucalyptus*	Semi-arid saline areas of Saurashtra, Gujarat	Production cycle 20 year, others like example 16.
45.	1 : 3.42	*Acacia catechu*	Doon valley, Uttar Pradesh, Tropical moist forest region	Plant spacing 4.55m × 4.55m other like example 8.
46.	1 : 4.00	*Eucalyptus*	Hill region, Ootacamund, Tamil Nadu	Plant spacing 2m × 2m, intensive research plantations, 10 years production cycle, green fodder grown on cover soil.
VI. *Returns over 400 per cent*				
47.	1 : 4.63	*Subabul*	South Maharashtra	Output when partly sold as poles, other like example 31.
48.	1 : 5.24	*Eucalyptus*	South Maharashtra	Plant spacing 2m × 1m, intensive irrigated cultivation, output partly sold as poles and rest as fuelwood, production cycle 5 years. farmers plantations.
49.	1 : 6.13	Poplars	Semi-arid, tropics, Haryana	Intensive irrigated plantation, fertilizing, weeding, plant protection, 8th year production cycle, secure marketing, plantations on farmers land.

7

SUMMING UP

The various studies conducted in India have emphasised on different aspects of rural energy situation ranging from the fuelwood supply and demand to the hard core problems being faced by the rural masses to get fuel within the reasonable approach. The reports of a number of committees set aside by the Government of India and some individual researchers have indicated about the severe fuelwood shortages by the beginning of the next century. The Planning Commission has estimated that the fuelwood availability would be one-third of its requirement by the turn of the century. There are no doubts in these speculations and the fact remains that the rural people have to face the harder times to come. Even in existing conditions the situation of wood availability in the forest predominated areas are far behind the expectations. Results of the surveys conducted in Garhwal area of Himalayas, show that the village women walk 10-12 kilometres every three or four days or even more frequently, to collect wood. They may even have to spend a night in the forest. In parts of Arunachal Pradesh, women used to collect four loads of firewood 20 years ago, only one can be collected now. In Chhatisgarh area on an average two persons spend 4–6 hours once in two days collecting fuelwood from forests. In Ganjam district the fuelwood collection has decreased from 125 quintals to 80 quintals per capita per year. The villagers not only cover a greater distance to collect wood–an average of 6.2 km today compared to 1.6 km in the past — they also collect a smaller quantity. In Chota Nagpur area, the women in the age group of 25–40 some times travel up to 10 miles to collect the firewood from the forests. Think about the fuelwood availability in the non-forest areas of the country?

The heavy burden on the drudgery rural people for fuelwood collection could not be removed unless fuelwood is not made available locally and comparatively cheap. Since land is a limited factor and agricultural lands are not be available for fuelwood plantations has emerged the thinking to develop the country's wastelands into fuelwood and fodder plantations. The programmes to develop these lands have seriously been taken up during the Sixth and Seventh Five Year Plans. The Prime Minister also has emphasised on a time bound programme for afforestation on the wastelands.

India's more than half of the geographical area (329 million hectares) is officially estimated to be in various stages of degradation and 50 million hectares of this are not being put to any productive use (Planning Commission, 1985) but although wasted, these lands have the potential for development. There has been a controversy over the actual area under wastelands in India. According to National Remote Sensing Agency's estimates 55.41 million hectares land fall under wastelands categories. Of these 12.77 million hectares form as unculturable waste (barren and rocky lands and snow cover and/or glacial lands) and the total culturable wastelands area accounts to about 42.64 million hectares. The Advisory Board on Energy (1985) estimates that at least 60 million hectares of land might be available for raising fuelwood/fodder plantations. The report further states that given the acute pressure on land and the other uses it could be put up to 50 per cent of the 60 million hectares actually under fuelwood/fodder plantations. The various experiments conducted during the last two — three decades in the country suggest that with the available technology, the wastelands can be reverted back to their original productive conditions through re-afforestation. Thus the parts of wasteland area of the country transcend both private and public ownership could be developed for various plantations, including fuelwood.

Recently National Wastelands Development Board and NRSA have prepared 2800 thematic maps on wastelands. These maps which cover 146 districts in 24 States of the country have more than 15 per cent of their total geographical area under wastelands. They interpret 13 categories of wastelands. The information is extremely useful for action plan at district level for reclamation of wastelands through afforestation, socio and farm forestry, soil conservation and land management practices. Since the wastelands fall in private hands & public lands, the strategies of development and management of these lands, thus, falling in both categories have to be dealt with separately. An integrated approach for coordinated and realistic programme is needed for the development of eco-systems on these wastelands. Whatever the future strategy is to be developed, it should be broad and comprehensive as well as multi-disciplinary, aiming not only at halting degradation but also increasing productivity on the wastelands.

Wastelands in India are under various degradation and to restore their productivity considerable inputs are required. The cost of reclamation depends on various factors like quality of the soil and its nutrient value, requirement of water, and the requirement of vegetation to be planted on it. Since the prevention of degradation or the restoration of degraded lands yield benefits over many years, a time horizon of 10-12 is considered suitable for such analysis (Das, 1984). The NABARD expects a rate of return within 15-20 years of afforestation projects in wastelands (Venketaraman, 1984). The *Usar* lands of Uttar Pradesh can be reclaimed for fuelwood afforestation at an expenditure of Rs. 10,000 per hectare. At a benefit cost ratio of 2.8, the pay back period will be ten years. The estimated cost of reclamation for Chambal ravines comes to Rs. 5,000 and at 4 benefit-cost ratio, the fuelwood plantations pay back period will also be 10 years (Chaturvedi, 1985).

Considering the different qualities of wastelands, part of these can be reclaimed for the suit of good agriculture and others can be put to growing fuelwood on any substantial scale. Abrol and Joshie (1984), estimated that the reclamation of alkali soils of the region of Uttar Pradesh, Haryana and Punjab will cost Rs. 5,325 per hectare suitable for field crop production. At a benefit-cost ratio of 1.29, the pay back period will be four years. Since both cost of reclamation and benefit-cost ratios varies for the development of wastelands under fuelwood afforestation and field crops, it requires a policy decision which land should be diverted for the wood lots. However, fuelwood plantations also require climate suitable for their growth. They need adequate moisture, moderate growing season and land where topography which is not too hostile and it has a few inches of good soil capable of retaining moisture. Fortunately, large areas satisfying the above conditions do exist in the wasteland tracks of the country. Having consider all these factors, the economic analysis of wasteland development would involve computation of benefits (market and extra market) and costs under the proposed conditions.

A very limited research based data are available where potential total increase in fuelwood production from reclaimed wastelands has been calculated. Further investigations are required in this direction for most suitable and promising species to be grown under different agro-climatic regions of the country. The steps taken by the Department of Non-Conventional Energy Sources through R & D and energy plantations projects would highlight on the actual local cost constraints of these plantations. But it is too early to make a comment on the subject since the projects are in the very early stages and plantations have suffered a lot due to recent drought conditions prevailed in the country.

Extension of the fuelwood plantations programme on degraded wastelands require huge sums of financial resources — both for the land development and planting process. The financial implications cover the nursery development, establishment and annual maintenance required to be invested during the period of plantations till the trees are available- to their end uses. the initial expenditure of fuelwood plantations on degraded lands is higher than on fertile soils (Chaturvedi, 1985). The economic returns are low but considering the fact these lands are of low value with poor productivity, the soil benefits through afforesting these lands are considerable. Fuelwood plantations on degraded wastelands provide extra market benefits like water and soil conservation and improving environment situation etc. which are difficult to express in strict monetary terms.

In absence of field data for most of the promising species of fuelwood, an assumption on certain cost constrains and their further calculations show that the per sapling raising expenses in the nurseries fall between 25 and 60 paise. Nurseries being the labour intensive units consume about half of the total cost as labour. The geographical location, sex availability of local labour force and species to be raised at the nurseries naturally have to affect on the cost of per sapling raised. In areas far from urban locations where other employment possibilities are low and labour is available in abundance on lower wages, the cost of nursery development will be lower. The variations in cost, thus have to be keep in mind while developing a large scale programme on the establishment of nurseries. Also it is not only the cost of sapling but the total initial expenditure on fuelwood plantations that accounts, about one-fourth of the total investment will require during the first year of plantation's establishment. The remaining three-fourth part of the expenditure is to be spreadover for the whole production cycle of the tree species.

There has been wide variations for the unit cost of plantations raised. A number of constraints are involved — conventional and high density agro-forestry, research and commercial plantations, type of wastelands and geographical locations of the plantations besides the various package of practices. For quick gain and to get rid of fuelwood shortages in the shortest period, decision has to be taken regarding the type of plantations to grow.

The experiences of high density agro-forestry show that high yields of fuelwood plantations are possible when they are planted with denser than conventional spacing and harvested on shorter than conventional cycles. The trees are allowed to make effective and maximum use of the entire plantation site, to remain sufficiently long to develop strong root system so as to permit repeated coppicing but they are not allowed to remain for unduly long time to complete with one another for space, sunlight, water and nutrients. *Eucalyptus, Prosopis juliflora* and *subabul* in parts of Gujarat and Maharashtra area and *Casuarine equisetifolia* in coastal belts of Tamil Nadu, Andhra Pradesh, Orissa and Pondicherry are being raised under HDAF on a large scale by individuals and also by the Forest Departments. The result of these plantations reveal that the cultural practices as followed are most effective in utilising solar energy. However, the planting density and cultural treatment are not yet standardised and a lost of work requires to be done in this direction.

The concept of high density agro-forestry as has been adopted by the growers, helps them to raise substantially their incomes. Unlike green revolution in farming, year round employment is available to the growers besides the risk of failure of a single plantation is minimized while growing fodder/grass species on the ground floor. The high cost of plantation where initial costs are comparatively high, could be managed through bank loaning as for crops loans. The HDAF plantations have also successfully been raised under the rainfed conditions with increased bio-mass but comparatively less than the irrigated plantations (Patel, 1988).

The various research results further advocate that the establishment of vegetation cover by fodder grasses along with the fuelwood species is one of the most effective ways to develop the wastelands into productivity ones. In most of the cases experiments proved the economic viability of the plantations carried out with grasses. Benefit-cost ratios are much favourable and plantations give the best economic propositions. Further considering the cost factor for such a large area of wastelands and for restoration of their permanent vegetal cover which are subject to soil and water erosion besides highly saline should be helped to regenerate themselves and to grow whatever grasses, shrubs or even weeds that they can sustain under natural conditions. This would by on means reduce the cost of reclamation of all the eroded wastelands. Like-wise a set of studies carried out suggest that if the species and technology is matched to site, fuelwood plantations besides economic considerations are the best for improving the local soil conditions. For example, *Acacia tortilis* coppies well and grows twice as fast as indigenous acacias and with stands arid conditions better than *Acacia nilotica, Acacia sengal* etc. is an excellent for soil stabilisation and barrier for the shifting of sand dunes in the arid zone of Rajasthan (Kaul & Gurumurthy, 1981).

An equally important aspect is of marketing. It is observed that under conventional plantation system, the fuelwoods in general are usually grown in conjunction with the more valuable parts of the tree i.e. the timber and the poles. In many parts of the country the farmers turned tree growers have to pay exorbitant marketing charges for their plants. For example, an average size of *eucalyptus* plant if marketed in a Punjab mandi costs Rs. 50 to the grower. (This includes the harvesting charges). Contrary to the fuelwood prices which have gone abnormally high during the last decade, there are at present very few buyers to the well grown eucalyptus timber plants (Patel 1988, Singh 1988 and Chaturvedi-personal discussions). Eucalyptus growers are facing problems for its disposal. This situation could only the possible to avoid that the plants should not be allowed to grow larger to become the timber. The high density agro-forestry in this regards will become a boon to the growers. The concept should be adopted as far as possible, at the nation level projects being taken up under the umbrella of social farm forestry programme.

Besides this, the emphasis on marketing channels and their cost for fuelwood require special attention if the fuelwood is produced on commercial basis. The Central as well as State Governments have to perform their prime role to establish the markets for fuelwood on regulated basis. This will exercise to stop the exploitation of fuelwood producers. Establishment of market outlets to improve the fuelwood distribution needs due weightage. This broadly includes organising marketing co-operatives, price structure, improvement in transport facilities, provision of fuelwood storages etc. etc.

As mentioned earlier, the wastelands fall under both the categories i.e. private ownership and public lands. The development of these lands for fuelwood plantations will involve many growers besides quite a large number of beneficiaries. Thus being a masses programme, the principle of fuelwood plantations must be imbued mentally and manually and the rural people (growers as well as consumers) should be involved to get their full participation. Quite a good amount of funds are being diverted for afforestation through NREP and RLEGP schemes. These have to be further strengthen not only for individual but to associate organisations (voluntary, financial, industrial etc.) and people of similar thinking with creative dedication shall also be involved in the programmes. There is *prime facie* need for motivating the farmers about the beneficial role of fuelwood plantations on the over all productivity of their farming. They must be educated that their salvation against energy crises lies only within their own hands. Thus fuelwood afforestation programme must be executed by the people themselves and for their own benefit and revamped institutions must actively assist them in this endeavour. In other worlds both wasteland development and fuelwood afforestation must not be attempted in isolation but as an integral part of the total efforts of rural development. The green revolution did not succeed only through poverty alleviation programme but through free enterprise. The benefits do procolate to others in due course. Unlike green revolution, fuelwood plantation concept can not be achieved without the farmers role in production and their self sufficiency in fuel, fodder and timber.

GLOSSARY OF TERMS

Afforestation : Forest established artificially on the land which previously did not carry forests.

Agro-forestry : A sustainable land management system which increases the yield of the land, combines the production of crops (including tree crops) and forest plants/or animals simultaneously or sequentially on the same unit of land and applied management practices that are compatible with the cultural practices of the local population.

Benefit-cost analysis : Technique for estimating the costs and returns from a production. Applied primarily to investment projects.

Biomass : Comprises all forms of matter derived from the biological activities taking place either on the surface of the soil or at different depths of the vast body of waterlakes, streams, rivers, seas and oceans.

Block Plantations : Planting of forestry trees in the fields – both as a pure cultivation or intercropped with the field crops.

Border Plantation : Planting of forestry trees on the boundaries of farm fields.

Canopy : The layer of tree crowns in a forest.

Commercial Energy : Sources of energy which are available after paying against money. These sources are channelled through proper marketing system, e.g. Coal, Petroleum, Electricity etc.

Community Forestry : Any situation which ultimately involves local people in a forestry activity.

Compounding : The process of calculating the interest on a principal amount (of money or resources) and all accumulated interest which that principal has earned over a specific period of time.

Coppice : The ability to regenerate by shoots or root suckers of trees coming out after cutting of the stem of the tree above the ground level or a forest so established.

Cost : See expenses.

Cost Benefit Ratio : Cost of production when measured in terms of total production benefits of the products.

Current Net Worth: It is the value of the assets minus the liabilities of the entire business.

Demand : The amount of commodity that households wish to purchase, the whole relation between the price and quantity demand.

Depreciation : The cost valuation of entire stock in the inventory for a specific period. The rate for depreciation is dependant not only on the prospective useful life of the property when acquired but also on the conditions under which it is used. The simplest method is the straight line method where the cost of the property minus its junk or scrap value is divided equally between the years of its estimated life.

Discounted Value : The calculated value today of a future payment (or receipt); This is the reverse of compounding.

Dung Cake : Sun dried cakes made of cow/buffaloe dung used extensively all over the country as a major source of energy in the villages.

Eco-systems : All the communities in a given area, considered together with their non-living environment. In general, an eco-system is a reasonably recognisable area, although adjacent eco-systems can overlap.

Energy Consumption ; Fuelwood consumption by multiplying by the calorific value of the fuel (MJ/kg) is converted into the units of energy consumption.

Environment : The surrounding condition and/or forces that influence or modify (i) the whole complex of climate edaphic and biotic factors that act upon an organism or an ecological community and ultimately determine its form and survival; and (ii) the aggregate of social and cultural condition that influence the life of an individual and community.

Expenses : The total of expenditure made on the different items for producing the farm/forest product. These can be for the imputed values as well as the actual cost of input items paid at the farm level.

Firewood : The terms 'firewood' and 'fuelwood' are generally used interchangeably, 'firewood' cannotes small-scale use such as for home cooking, whereas 'fuelwood' implies large scale industrial use.

Fuel Consumption : The amount of fuel consumed during the cooking. For this measurement, the fuel available to the cook is pre-weighted and fuel remaining upon the completion of the meal is weighted in order to obtain the consumption during cooking.

Gross Income : Gross income is the total value of the farm produce (including forest plants) whether sold or disposed of in any other manner e.g. given in kind as wages, consumed at home etc. It concludes the money obtained for produce actually sold and the value of the reminder at the harvest prices prevalent in the locality.

Habitat : A place where a plant or animal species naturally grows and lives i.e. purely the physical environment of a locality occupied by a living group.

Humus : Partly decayed plant matter in the soil.

Internal Rate of Return : The internal rate of return of a project is the rate of interest which, when used to discount the future cash flows back to the presently results in the discounted income being exactly equal to the discounted costs. In other words, the internal rate of return represents the financial yield or profitability of a project in terms of a percentage rate of interest.

Leaching : The removal of soluble compounds by the down ward percolation of water through the soil.

Man-made Forests: Forests crops raised artificially either by sowing or planting. Such forests include; afforestation, re-afforestation and artificial regeneration. Man made forests thus include plantations raised for increasing the productivity of forests.

Moisture Content (m.c.) : Is the ratio of the weight of the moisture in the wood to the weight of dry wood.

$$\text{m.c.} = \frac{\text{wet weight} - \text{dry weight}}{\text{dry weight}} \times 100$$

Mulching : A technique used to reduce water evaporation from soil, to provide aeration in the root zone and to reduce weeds.

Net Income/Profit or Loss : Net Income or loss represents the difference between the gross income and expenditure.

Nitrogen fixing : The conversion of elemental nitrogen (N_2) from the atmosphere to organic forms utilizable in biological processes.

Non-Commercial Energy : Sources of energy available for its supply without paying cash e.g. dung cake, firewood, agricultural waste etc.

Nutrients : Six essential ingredients of an organisms growth and supply of energy; carbohydrates, fats, proteins, water, salts and vitamins.

Photosynthesis : The production of organic compounds such as glucose, from carbon dioxide and water with the aid of light and chlorophyll, and liberation of oxygen.

Production Forestry : The practice of forestry aims at producing timber and wood for industrial uses.

Re-afforestation : Forests established artificially on the lands which carried forests earlier.

Silviculture : The theory and practice of controlling the establishment, composition, and growth of forests.

Species : Two individuals belong to the same species if they will enter-breed in the wild and produce live off spring that are themselves fertile. This definition does break down in many cases, however, and a definition that covers all cases is actually impossible.

Social Benefit : The package of overall benefits that are received by the society (as opposed to an individual) from a production/project.

Social costs : The cost of a society (as against an individual) incurs when its resources are used to produce a given commodity.

Social Forestry : The practice of forestry in all its aspects on farms and village lands generally integrated with other farm operations.

Strip plantations : Tree cultivation programme taken up on the sides of railways, roads, canals, rivers etc. Strip plantation is some time called as linear plantation.

Stumpage : Net value of the tree before harvesting, determined by subtracting from the market value of the product the cost of harvesting, haulage and sale in the market place – it is therefore, equivalent to the value of the tree if sold standing.

Vegetable Waste : Residues of field crops (tops, roots, shoots, barks etc.) generally used for burning as a source of the energy.

Wastelands : The team is being used as a synonym of degraded lands. It is a general term which includes any type of land, irrespective of its ownership, which is producing less than 20 per cent of its optimum biological productivity.

Yield : The rate of return on an investment. Production per unit of area.

BIBLIOGRAPHY

Abrol, I.P. and Gill, H.S. (1984), Afforestation of Salt Affected Soils, *Convention and Symposium of the Bio-Energy Society of India,* New Delhi.

Abrol, I.P. and Joshi P.K. (1984), Economic Viability of Reclamation of Alkali lands with special reference to Agriculture and Forestry, *Seminar Proceeding, SPWD,* New Delhi.

Agarwala, V.P. (1985), *Forests in India*, Oxford & IBH Publishing Co., New Delhi.

Astra, (1981), Rural Energy Consumption Pattern – A Field Survey; Centre for the Application of Science & Technology to Rural Areas, Indian Institute of Science, Bangalore.

BAIF, *Journal, Bhartiya Agro-Industries Foundation*, Uralikanchan, Pune.

Bantley, W. (1984); The Uncultivated Half, *USAID Report*, Ford Foundation, New Delhi.

Bhumla, D.R. and Arvind Khare; Estimates of Wastelands in India, Society for Promotion of Wastelands Development, New Delhi.

Central, Statistical Organisation, Ministry of Planning, GOI, (1985), *Statistical Abstracts*, New Delhi.

Central Statistical Organisation, Ministry of Planning, Monthly Abstract of Statistics (various volumes), New Delhi, Govt. of India.

Centre for Science and Environment (1986); Developing India's Wasted lands – A briefing Paper, New Delhi.

Chandra, J.P. (1986); Poplar – A Cash Crop for North Indian Farmers, *Indian Forester*, August 1986, p.668-70.

Chatha, I.S. etc. (1987), Production and Marketing of Eucalyptus in Punjab, *Department of Economics,* Punjab Agricultural University, Ludhiana.

Chaturvedi, A.N. (1982), Poplar Farming in U.P., India, *U.P. Forest Bulletin 45,* Lucknow.

Chaturvedi, A.N. (1983), Eucalyptus for Farming, *U.P. Forest Bulletin 48,* Lucknow.

Chaturvedi, A.N. (1985), Firewood on Degraded Lands, *U.P. Forest Bulletin 50,* Lucknow.

Chopra, S.K. (1988), Rural Energy – Integrated Approach Vital; Survey of Indian Agriculture 1988, *The Hindu*, Madras, pp. 21-27.

Das, D.C. (1984), Benefits from Soil and Water Conservation Programme – A State of fact Paper. *S.P.W.D., Seminar Proceedings,* New Delhi.

Directorate of Economics & Statistics, Ministry of Agriculture, G.O.I. (1985), *Indian Agriculture in Brief,* New Delhi.

El-Hinnawi, E. (1983), National Activities and Trends in New and Renewable Sources of Energy; Tycooly International Publishers Ltd., Dublin.

F.A.O. (1983), Wood Fuel Surveys, Forestry for Local Community Development Programme, Rome.

F.A.O. (1985), Wood for Energy; *Forestry Topics Report, No.1,* Rome.

F.A.O.; Year Book of Forest Products, various volumes, Rome.

Foley, Gerald (1986), Economics of Fuelwood Substitutes, *Unasylva,* Vol. 38, (153), p. 15.

Forest Research Institute and Colleges (1985), Information on Important Tree Species, Dehradun.

Gadgil, M. *et al.* (1982), Forest Management in India – A Critical Review; Centre for Monitoring Indian Economy, Bombay.

Govt. of India (1984): Centrally Sponsored Scheme – Social Forestry including Rural Fuelwood Plantation, Ministry of Agriculture, New Delhi.

Govt. of India (1985), The Advisory Board on Energy, *Report*, New Delhi.

Gupta, D.D. and Gangwar, A.C. (1986); Profitability of Crops in Haryana, *Farm Management Extension Bulletin,* No.2, Haryana Agricultural University, Hissar.

Khan, I. (1987), *Wastelands Afforestation,* Oxford and IBH Publishing Company Pvt. Ltd., New Delhi.

Gupta, T. (1979) Economics of Energy Plantation in the Arid Region in India, *Research Planning Workshop on Energy for Rural Development,* Ahmedabad.

Hedge, N.G. (1987), Hand Book of Wastelands Development, Bhartiya Agro-Industries Foundation, Pune.

Hegde N.G. and Abhyankar. P.D. (1985); The Greening of Wastelands, Proceedings of Workshop on Utilization of Wastelands for Bio-Energy, edited, Pune.

Hindustan Times, New Delhi.

I C A R, (1966); Hand Book of Agriculture, New Delhi.

Kalla, J.C. *et al.* (1975), Economics of Commercial Fuel Plantation Crops in Arid Zone of Rajasthan, *Agriculture Situation in India*, 30: 241-44.

Kalla, J.C. *et al.* (1978), Techno-Economic felling cycle for Selected Energy Plantation Species in Arid Areas of Western Rajasthan, *Annals of Arid zone*, 17 : 42-51

Kalla, J.C. (1988), Forestry and Economic Development, *Indian Journal of Agricultural Economics*, Vol. 43(3), pp. 237-257.

Kaul, R.N., Gurumurthy, K. (1981), Planting for Energy, *Science Today*, 15(10) : 43-46.

Manjoor Alam *et al.* (1985), Fuelwood in Urban Markets, Hyderabad.

Mann, H.S. and Muthana K.D. (1984), Arid Zone Forestry; Central Arid Zone Research Institute, Jodhpur.

Mathur, H.N. *et al* (1979), Benefit – Cost Ratios for Fuel cum Fodder Plantation in Doon Valley, *Indian Joun, Soil Conserve*, 7(2); 53-58.

Mathur, R.K. (1984), Economics of Agro-Forestry for Wasteland Reclamation, *Seminar Proceedings, SPWD,* New Delhi.

Mathur, R.S. *et al.* (1984), Price Trends of Firewood in Haryana, *The Indian Forester,* Vol. 110(10), p. 973.

Mishra D.N. (1988), Guide to Tree Planting in Uttar Pradesh, Society for Promotion of Wastelands Development, New Delhi.

Mohindra, V. (1973), Economics of Eucalyptus Plantations in Punjab, *Forestry Conference*, Dehradun.

National Academy of Sciences (1980); Firewood Crops: Shrub and Tree Species for Energy Production, Washington, D.C.

National Commission on Agriculture (1976), Abridged Report, Ministry of Agriculture, Government of India, New Delhi.

Natrajan I. (1980), Composition Pattern of Cooking Energy in North India; National Council of Applied Economic Research, New Delhi.

Noach, D. and Fruhwald, A. (1982), Consequences of the Energy and Raw Material Crisis for the Raw Material Wood; Natural Resources and Development Vol. 16 p. 7-26.

NWDB (1985), Wastelands Development Programme: Guidelines for Action; Ministry of Environment and Forests, Govt. of India, New Delhi.

NWDB (1987), Nursery Manual for Species Commonly used in Social Forestry in India, New Delhi.

NWDB (Undated), Progress Report, New Delhi.

Operations Research Group (1988), Energy Plantation in Wastelands – The case of Kutch, *ORG Report*, Baroda.

Pant, M.M. (1980), Economics and Social Costs and Benefits of Forestry in Tropical Region, *Eleventh Common Wealth Forestry – Conference*, London.

Pant, M.M. (1984), Forest Economics and Valuation, Natraj Publications, Dehradun.

Patel, *et al.* (1982) Economics of Wood Energy in India, *Urja* : 313-21.

Patel, K.B. (1987), Experiments with *Prosopis juliflora* at Adarsh Farm Vatva, Ahmedabad, *Kisan World*, p. 35.

Patel, V.J. (1983); High Density Eucalyptus Plantation in Bhavnagar District, *Indian Forester* Vol. 109.

Patel, V.J. (1986), Wastelands Development for Bio-mass, *The Greening of Wastelands Seminar Proceedings*, BAIF, Poona.

Patel V.J. (1988), A New Strategy for High Density Agro-Forestry, Jivrajbhai Patel Agro-Forestry Centre, Kardej, Gujarat.

Planning Commission, Govt. of India (1979) Report of the Working Group on Energy Policy, New Delhi.

Planning Commission, Govt. of India, (1982), Report of the Fuelwood Study Committee, New Delhi.

Prasad, SSR *et al.* (1988); Management of Fuelwood around Urban Centres; Paper submitted to *Bio-Energy Symposium*, Baroda, 1988.

Puri, D.N. and Khybri, M.L. (1975), Economics of Chambal Ravines Afforestation, *Indian Forester* 101 (8) : 448-451.

Puri, D.N. and Singh, J.P. (1977) Economic Utilization of Ravines for Fuel cum Fodder, *Annual Report, CSWCRTI*, Dehradun, U.P.

Ram Babu *et al.* (1982), Economics and Benefit Cost Ratio of the Eucalyptus plantation for Fuel Purposes in Denuded lands of Doon Valley, *Van Vigyan*, 20 (1 and 2): 1-4.

Ram Prakash and Drake Hocking (1986): Some Favourite Trees for Fuel Fodder; Society for Promotion of Wastelands Development (SPWD), New Delhi.

Rao, K.S. (1987), Energy Plantation for Power Generation, *Proceedings of Bio-Energy*, Udaipur, 272.

Reddy, A. D.N. and Reddy, B.S. (1983), Energy in a Society – Case study of Fire wood in Bangalore; *Economic and Political Weekly*, Vol. XVIII (4).

Relwani, R.R. and Hegde, N.G. (1986), Economics of Subabul, *BAIF Journal*, $(4).

Relwani, R.R. (1981), Studies on the value of Kababul for Fodder and Wood Production, Seminar on *Ipll-ipll*, Gujarat State Forest Department, Gandhi Nagar.

Sharma, H.S. (1980), *Ravine Erosion in India*, Concept Publishing Ltd., New Delhi.

Singh, Bakshish (1972), Economics of Afforestation in Ravine Lands, *Symposium on Man-made Forests in India*, Dehradun : 26-32.

Singh, Kamla *et al.* (1988) Poplar (*Poplar deltoides*) in Forest and Agro-Forestry System, *Indian Forester*, November 1988, p. 814-817.

Singh, Har Swarup (1988), Comparative Economics of Trees and Crop Production in Haryana, *Indian Journal of Agricultural Economics*, Vol. 43 (3) pp. 289-295.

Sondhi, M. (1984), Farmer's View Point, *Seminar Proceedings; Economics of Wastelands*, SPWD, New Delhi.

S.P.W.D. (1984), Economics of Wastelands Development; *SPWD/NABARD Seminar*, New Delhi.

S.P.W.D., *Wasteland News*, Quarterly News Letter of S.P.W.D., New Delhi.

Srivastava B.P. and Pant, M.M. (1979), Social Forestry on a Cost-Benefit Analysis Framework, *Indian Forester*, 105 : 2-25.

Subbayyan, R. and Chittaranjan (1982), Fodder cum Fuel plantation in the black cotton soils of Bellary under rainfed conditions, *Annual Report, CSWCRTI*, Dehradun, U.P.

United Nations: *Monthly Bulletin of Statistics*, various volumes, New York.

Venkataraman, K.G. (1984); Designing, Planning and Financing of Tree Projects Over Wastelands, *S.P.W.D. Seminar Proceedings*, New Delhi.

Vimal Kishore *et al.* (1982), Economics of Fuel cum Fodder Plantation in Mahi ravines of Gujarat State, *Annual Report CSWCRTI*, Dehradun, U.P.

Vimal, O.P. and Tyagi P.D. (1986), *Fuelwood from Wastelands*, Yatan Publications, Delhi.

Vishawanathan, M.K. *et al.* (1982), Economics Utilisation of Class V, VI Lands for Fuel and Fodder Plantation in Dehradun, *Annual Report, CSWCRTI*, Dehradun, U.P.

Vohra, B.B. (1978), Managing India's Land and Water Resources, Government of India, New Delhi.

Yadav, J.P.S. (1980); Salt affected Soils and their Afforestation, *Indian Forester*, 106 4), 259-72.

INDEX